Elections and Voting Behaviour
in Britain

CONTEMPORARY POLITICAL STUDIES

Series Editor: John Benyon, *University of Leicester*

A series which provides authoritative and concise introductory accounts of key topics in contemporary political studies.

Other titles in the series include:

Pressure Groups, Politics and Democracy in Britain
W. GRANT, *University of Warwick*

UK Political Parties Since 1945
Edited by ANTHONY SELDON, *Institute of Contemporary British History*

The Constitution in Question
Edited by JOHN BENYON, *University of Leicester*

CONTEMPORARY POLITICAL STUDIES

Elections and Voting Behaviour in Britain

DAVID DENVER

University of Lancaster

Philip Allan
New York London Toronto Sydney Tokyo Singapore

First published 1989 by
Philip Allan
66 Wood Lane End, Hemel Hempstead,
Hertfordshire, HP2 4RG
A division of
Simon & Schuster International Group

© D.T. Denver, 1989

Printed and bound in Great Britain by
Billing and Sons Ltd, Worcester

Library of Congress Cataloging-in-Publication Data

Denver, D.T.
  Elections and voting behaviour in Britain/David Denver.
    p. cm.
    ISBN 0-86003-411-9. — ISBN 0-86003-711-8 (pbk.)
    1. Elections — Great Britain. 2. Voting — Great Britain.
I. Title.
JN956.D46   1989
324.941—dc20   89-6870
                                      CIP

British Library Cataloguing in Publication Data

Denver, D.T. (David Trodden), *1944–*
  Elections and voting behaviour in Britain.
  (Contemporary political studies)
  1. Great Britain. Electorate. Voting
  behaviour
  I. Title II. Series
  324.941

  ISBN 0-86003-411-9
  ISBN 0-86003-711-8 pbk

---

2 3 4 5   93 92 91 90

Contents

Preface

Elections in Britain, as in all liberal democracies, are central to the political process. They involve, to some extent, almost the entire adult population and inform almost every aspect of political life. Not surprisingly, interest in elections is also widespread — from students and teachers of British politics at school or undergraduate level to journalists, members of political parties and many otherwise 'ordinary' people. The problem for people like these is that in recent years the specialised literature dealing with elections and voting behaviour in Britain has grown enormously and has become highly technical and statistically complex.

My intention in this book is to introduce readers to this wider literature in a way that is as non-technical as I can make it. I hope that there is enough 'meat' in the book to satisfy undergraduates and A-level students but I hope, too, that those whose interest in the subject is more general will find the book rewarding. With this audience in mind, I have had to simplify some rather complicated material and I apologise in advance to any of the authors discussed who may think that I have oversimplified their arguments, theories or conclusions. *Really* serious students of electoral analysis must consult the primary literature themselves.

Talking about, reading about, observing, participating in and even doing research on elections is not just for 'serious students', however. If any readers who are not currently students acquire from this book a fuller understanding of trends in British elections and a keener, more critical interest in the electoral process, then it will have served one of its major purposes.

Preparing the book has, of course, involved me in numerous debts.

I am grateful to the following for permission to reproduce material: American Enterprise Institute, Butterworth Scientific Ltd, Cambridge University Press, David Butler, Ivor Crewe, Patrick Dunleavy, Anthony Heath and William Miller. In addition, Anthony Heath kindly provided me with unpublished data from the BES (British Election Study) survey of the 1987 general election.

Jeremy Mitchell commented helpfully on an early draft of the manuscript and John Bochel also gave me the benefit of his sage advice. Russell Price, with his enviable eye for detail, made numerous useful suggestions on points of style. I am especially grateful to my colleague Gordon Hands, who read and re-read numerous drafts and with whom I have had lengthy and profitable discussions at every stage of writing. The general editor of the series, John Benyon, and Philip Cross of Philip Allan Publishers Ltd, were valued sources of encouragement and advice. Finally, my wife Barbara not only supported, encouraged and tolerated a good deal, but also mastered a new word-processing system to prepare the manuscript.

Despite the best efforts of all of these, there remain, no doubt, errors of interpretation and (just possibly!) fact. Responsi' ility for these is mine.

David Denver
Lancaster 1989

1

The Study of Elections and Electoral Behaviour

Why study elections?

Elections are fun. In the first half of the nineteenth century, part of the fun involved the voters getting roaring drunk at the candidates' expense, brawling in the street with opponents and pelting them with rotten fruit. The practice of candidates 'treating' voters was effectively ended by the Second Reform Act of 1867 which greatly enlarged the electorate. There were now simply too many voters to treat. In addition, in 1872 the Ballot Act made voting secret (previously voters had to declare their choice in public) so that candidates could no longer check that the voters they had treated actually voted for them. Finally, in 1883, the Corrupt Practices Act outlawed treating (much to the disappointment of most voters, one suspects).

Despite this, elections continued to be a form of public entertainment until well into the twentieth century. In 1922 a crowd of 10,000 assembled to hear the declaration of the general election result in Dundee and were rewarded with the news that the sitting member, Winston Churchill, had been defeated by a Prohibitionist!

Today, elections continue to be enjoyed by all sorts of people. Candidates and party workers often experience a sense of exhilaration during campaigns; people in the media are caught up in the excitement of reporting a major national event; television presenters get to use all sorts of computer gadgetry; pollsters, analysts and pundits find themselves

1

in great demand. Even the mass of ordinary voters, who now largely 'spectate' on election campaigns, appear to enjoy the 'horse race', some of them betting on the outcome and many watching campaign reports and party broadcasts on television. Election night parties are not uncommon.

Studying elections is also fun. Some people collect stamps, some are train spotters, others pore over cricket statistics in *Wisden*. But there are also 'election buffs' around the country who collect, collate and analyse election results.

Part of the fascination is the sheer mass of information available. In general elections there are results for 650 constituencies to be looked at, but in addition there are elections to the European Parliament and elections for local councils, which involve many thousands of wards and electoral divisions. Local election results in Britain are not centrally collected and published by the state so that even acquiring a comprehensive collection of results becomes an interesting exercise in detective work.

Election results are also fascinating because they are numerical in form and numbers can be analysed endlessly. Voting figures can be aggregated, averaged, graphed and used to construct maps. Some academic studies of electoral behaviour take statistical manipulation so far that they become incomprehensible to all but about a hundred people in the whole country! But a great deal can be done with just a few elementary techniques.

The fact that elections yield masses of quantitative data amenable to statistical analysis, together with the rapid development of computers, partly explains the huge growth in the academic literature on elections over the past 25 years or so. But there's more to it than that. Elections are studied because they are important.

Most people would agree that it is the existence of free, competitive elections which distinguishes political systems that we normally call 'democratic' from others. Different versions of democratic theory attach different weights to elections and assign them different functions, but all see elections as central to democracy.

In traditional democratic theory, elections give sovereignty or ultimate power to the citizens. It is via elections that the citizen participates in the political process and ultimately determines the personnel and policies of governments. Only a government which is elected by the people is a legitimate government. Other democratic theorists view elections as only one among a number of channels of citizen influence, and stress the indirect nature of influence through the electoral process. Other theories suggest that elections simply allow citizens a choice between competing élites. The existence of free elections remains, none the less, the essential difference between democratic and non-democratic states. Even theories such as Marxism, which wish to deny that elections permit the people to have any real influence over the state, nevertheless agree that elections are important means of binding people to the political system by creating, in the Marxists' view, an illusion of influence.

Exactly how and how much elections affect what governments do is, then, a matter of some debate. At a minimum, however, it is clear that they provide a peaceful way of changing governments (and this is not unimportant given the number of governments around the world that are removed by violence). They also make governments accountable to the electorate, at least once every five years in Britain. Voters can pass judgement on the government and either keep it in office or replace it.

Elections are, therefore, the means by which the great mass of citizens can participate directly in the political process, and in Britain millions of citizens do participate in this way. For most, voting is the only overtly political action which is regularly undertaken.

Undeniably, general elections are major national events which precipitate greatly increased political activity, discussion, interest and media coverage. On election night, crowds gather in Trafalgar Square and the attention of almost the whole nation is at least partly engaged by the election. Next day, the front pages of all newspapers are entirely devoted to election news.

These would be reasons enough for studying elections. But it is also clear that elections do make a difference to what happens. Although there might be some debate about the precise extent or importance of the difference made when one party rather than another wins an election, it seems to strain credulity to suggest, for example, that the Conservative victory in the 1979 general election has had little effect on subsequent events.

Elections, then, are central to democracy, occasion mass political behaviour, determine who governs and thus affect the lives of all of us. By studying them we seek to deepen our understanding of how a key process of democracy operates, to discover how citizens make their voting decisions and to explain election outcomes.

In this book I discuss some of the major themes that have emerged from studies of British elections and electoral behaviour. The literature on this topic is vast, detailed and sometimes technically complex. It is necessary, therefore, to paint with rather broad brush strokes. I hope, however, that readers will gain an enhanced understanding of recent developments in this important area of national political life, and perhaps also acquire the enthusiasm to pursue the subject in more detail elsewhere.

As a preliminary, however, since even a basic understanding of election results inevitably involves dealing with numerical data, the remainder of this chapter is devoted to an explanation of some of the statistical techniques which are commonly used in electoral analysis.

Analysing election results

As I noted above, election results are quantitative in form. They yield masses of data. Any book or article about elections and voting behaviour will almost certainly contain some statistics. In order to appreciate this literature fully or to undertake analysis on one's own, it is important to have a basic grasp of the nature of different kinds of data and of some elementary statistical techniques.

Types of data

Figure 1.1 differentiates between four types of data according to *level* and *scale* of measurement.[1]

Firstly, what does level of data mean? *Aggregate*-level data are data which refer to an aggregate or collectivity. We know, for example, that in the Lancaster constituency in the 1987 general election there was a 79.2 per cent turnout and the distribution of votes was 46.7 per cent Conservative, 32.4 per cent Labour and 19.9 per cent Alliance. This result was obtained by totting up, or aggregating, the number of people who voted and the party they voted for. From the final result we do not know how any individual voted but we do know something about the

Scale Level	Aggregate	Individual
Interval	a	c
Nominal	b	d

Figure 1.1 Types of data

collectivity of voters in the constituency. It is an important feature of aggregate data that they cannot be used to infer anything about the behaviour or characteristics of individuals. Other examples of aggregate data are the percentage of council tenants in a ward, the number of unemployed people in a constituency, the percentage of manual workers in the North of England and the change in Labour's share of the vote between 1983 and 1987 over the country as a whole.

If, however, I had organised a sample survey in the Lancaster constituency I would have sent out interviewers to ask questions of individual voters. By asking the right questions we could find exactly what the individuals in the sample did in the election. This would yield *individual*-level data.

Turning now to scale of measurement, *interval*-scale data are pieces of numerical information that can be plotted on a scale which has a number of fixed points, each an equal distance apart. A person's height, for example, is measured in a precise number of feet and inches (or is it metres and centimetres these days?). More relevant from our point of view, anything that can be expressed as a percentage is on an interval scale going from 0 to 100. *Nominal*-scale data, on the other hand, are pieces of information that can only be assigned to one among a number of categories. The categories are discrete and do not imply any ascending or descending scale. Thus, 'party voted for' is nominal. A person votes Conservative, Labour, SLD or something else and these are categories rather than points on a scale. The same is true of sex, religion, occupation, ethnic group, type of housing, opinion on nuclear weapons and so on.

Matters like these about which we have information — whether related to individuals or constituencies — are known as 'variables'. These are simply things that vary. Thus sex, religion and opinions vary from person to person. Similarly, turnout and party shares of the vote vary from constituency to constituency and from one election to another. Generally, in electoral analysis some variables are thought of as *dependent*, that is their variation is caused or influenced by something else. The dependent variable — an individual's vote or the share of the vote obtained by a party, for example — is what is to be explained. *Independent* variables are factors which do the explaining. Thus if we take the variables sex and vote, it is possible that sex might explain vote — vote is dependent — but hard to conceive of a person's vote influencing his or her sex!

Characteristically, individual data are of the nominal type and aggregate data are interval-scale. In other words, the cells indicated 'a' and 'd' in Figure 1.1 are the commonest forms of data. But data that would fit into cells 'b' and 'c' are also found. Thus, constituencies could be categorised according to the party which holds them ('b') or individuals could be given a score out of teh on a series of questions testing political knowledge ('c').

None the less, for the sake of clarity my discussion of interval-scale data analysis will be confined to aggregate data and, in the next section, I will treat nominal data as survey-derived data.

Sample surveys and the analysis of nominal data

Individual-level data relevant to the study of voting behaviour are normally collected by means of sample surveys. I do not propose to discuss here the statistical basis of sampling or the various kinds of sample.[2] It is enough for students of voting behaviour to know that, given an appropriate sample, electoral analysts can make statements about the population from which the sample was taken with a certain margin of error and 'level of confidence'. The reliability and accuracy of survey results varies with the type and size of sample used. As a rule of thumb, however, in reputable studies it is usually highly probable (95 per cent certain) that a sample figure will be within two or three points either way of the true figure for the population as a whole. For example, if an appropriate survey found that 40 per cent of *Sun* readers voted Conservative in 1983 (which is, in fact, what was found by Dunleavy and Husbands 1985, p. 113) then it can be shown that it is 95 per cent certain that among all *Sun* readers the proportion who voted Conservative was 40 per cent plus or minus about three points (i.e. between 37 and 43 per cent).

The important point to note is that figures derived from surveys should not be regarded as precisely accurate. They are *estimates* of the true situation among the population being studied. Put another way, surveys are liable to sampling error, a fact which authors sometimes forget when they become carried away with the apparent precision of the figures produced from their surveys.

Surveys are also liable to other sources of error. Questions may be ambiguous or unclear, lead respondents to give particular answers, or be interpreted by the respondents in a way that was not intended by the questionnaire designer. Mistakes may be made by interviewers in recording answers; slips happen during the tedious operations of converting answers to numbers and transferring them to a computer. Even so, sample surveys are generally reliable and powerful research tools. They have become an indispensable part of electoral analysis and have played a crucial role in advancing our understanding of electoral behaviour.

Academic survey studies of voting behaviour were pioneered in the 1940s in the United States. The first survey of voting behaviour in Britain was a local study carried out in the constituency of Greenwich in 1950 (Benney et al. 1956). Further local surveys followed in the 1950s but it was not until 1963 that the first national survey study was undertaken under the direction of David Butler and Donald Stokes (Butler and Stokes 1969). Although 1963 was not an election year, this was the first of a series of national surveys carried out at every general election since 1964 under the auspices of the British Election Study (BES). The results of all these surveys are held on computer at the social science data archive at Essex University and researchers in the field can get copies of the data files. These are a real treasure trove and have formed the basis of numerous books and scholarly articles dealing with voting in Britain.

National surveys are expensive, however (indeed the BES survey of the 1983 general election obtained the necessary funding only at the last minute). There have been and continue to be lots of more limited surveys. Researchers have surveyed voters in particular localities and specific groups of voters such as women, 'affluent workers', young people and members of ethnic minority groups.

A public opinion poll is a type of survey, as are the 'exit' polls regularly conducted for television channels at by-elections and general elections.[3] Like academic surveys, these polls produce a great deal of individual data. Most people pay attention to political polls only at election time, when they achieve high visibility by giving almost daily figures for the voting intentions of the electorate. They have, indeed, become an important and controversial feature of modern election campaigns (see Chapter 5). In fact, however, polls monitor the opinions of the electorate continuously. The Gallup organisation, for example, produces a regular monthly report which, in addition to current voting intention figures, records details of the voters' perceptions of party leaders, government performance, current issues and much else.

Polling firms are, of course, commercial organisations. They are not particularly interested in obtaining the kind of detailed information about voting choice and the factors affecting it that academics are. Poll interviews tend, therefore, to be much shorter than interviews for major academic surveys — often being conducted in the street — and the information sought from voters is normally confined to a few obvious attributes such as age, sex, housing tenure and occupation. None the less, polls constitute a valuable source of individual data. They provide regular monthly data and their results are analysed and published very rapidly. A few days after the 1987 general election, commentators were able to use poll results to discuss voting patterns in the election. In contrast, it takes months if not years for reports on major academic surveys to become available.

As noted above, surveys can be used to obtain both nominal- and interval-scale data about individuals. Typically, however, nominal-scale data are more commonly derived from surveys. Normally, the first step in analysing data of this kind is to ascertain *frequency distributions*. This simply means determining how many survey respondents fall into each of the nominal categories being used. For convenience, the numbers are usually converted to percentages. An example is given in Table 1.1, which shows (almost) the full range of answers given when respondents to the 1983 BES survey were asked how they had voted in the general election.

It will be noticed, firstly, that the percentages have been rounded to whole numbers. Since surveys involve only samples of the population, results based on them are estimates of the true figure for the population and there is, therefore, little point in giving the results to two decimal places! Secondly, the number of cases upon which the percentages are based is shown in the table (N = 3,955). This is good practice since percentages based on small numbers (or Ns) are inherently unreliable. The sample size in this case is very large — polling firms usually use a national sample of about 1,200 people in order to generalise about the British electorate.

Single-variable analysis of this kind does not take us very far. Usually we want to investigate the relationship between two or more variables. In this case, for example, we might want to test the hypothesis that party choice (the dependent variable) is affected by whether people have manual

Table 1.1　Vote in 1983 (%)

Did not vote	Con.	Lab.	Alliance	Liberal	SDP	Others	Refused to say
17	36	24	11	7	2	1	2 (N = 3,955)

Source: BES data.

or non-manual occupations (the independent variable). This is certainly not an original hypothesis but it will serve to illustrate how relationships of this kind are investigated. This is done by constructing *cross-tabulations* or *contingency tables*.

The idea behind cross-tabulation is not difficult to grasp. We have eight categories of response to a question on voting and all respondents are assigned to a category. We now divide respondents additionally into one of the six categories into which their occupations were coded. There are now 48 potential categories (8 × 6) into which individuals may be allocated, and each respondent is put into one of them by, as it were, looking first at how they voted and then at their occupational status. If this were done by hand it would take a long time. It is not so long, in fact, since cross-tabulations were created using punched cards and a machine called a card-sorter or even, strange as it may seem, knitting needles! But now computers produce tables in seconds.

When presented in the form of a table, the categories constitute the *cells* of the table. A table of 48 cells would be very large and difficult to read, however, and so it is important to try to simplify the data for presentation. It seems sensible in this case, for example, to start by combining the separate Alliance, Liberal and SDP categories, since we are not (for the purposes of this analysis) interested in any differences between them. It also helps if we omit cells containing information which is not needed for the particular topic being investigated. Thus, I can exclude respondents who did not vote, voted 'other' or refused to say how they voted. Considering the independent variable, occupation, respondents who for one reason or another could not be assigned to the manual or the non-manual category can be left out. This leaves us with a table of just six cells. It is standard practice to combine categories and to present only selected cells of tables in this way. There will always be categories for respondents who have failed to answer a question, or given an unintelligible answer, which can be omitted; otherwise, the selection depends upon the particular question being investigated.

The reduced cross-tabulation of party choice by occupational class is shown in Table 1.2. The exclusion of some cells has reduced the original number of respondents from 3,955 to 2,989. The table shows that there is a clear relationship between type of occupation and vote in 1983, much as we would expect. Non-manual (white-collar) workers are more likely to vote Conservative and less likely to vote Labour than are manual workers. There is less difference between the two groups in respect of propensity to vote for the Alliance.

Table 1.2 Party choice by occupational class, 1983 (%)

	Non-manual	Manual
Conservative	55	35
Labour	17	44
Alliance	28	22
	($N = 1,567$)	($N = 1,422$)

Source: BES data.

The percentages shown in the table are, as I have explained, estimates from a sample of the electorate. We need to know, therefore, whether the differences found in the sample are likely to reflect real differences among the population at large. To discover this, tests of statistical significance are normally applied. These are rather complicated (see Startup and Whittaker 1982, Ch. 9) but frequently authors simply report that what they have found is 'significant at the 95 per cent level' or 'p < 0.05'. This means that there is only a 5 per cent chance, or a probability of less than 0.05, that the difference found in the sample does not reflect a difference in the population as a whole. In other words, the difference found is statistically significant: it is not due to chance.

The information contained in Table 1.2 could have been presented in another way. Instead of using the number of people in each occupational group as the basis for calculating the percentages, I could have used the numbers who voted for each party. Table 1.3 shows how the data look if this is done.

It must be emphasised that the numbers which were originally in the cells of Table 1.3 are exactly the same as those used to construct Table 1.2. It is simply that the percentages have been calculated on different bases. The two tables tell us different things. Table 1.2 tells us how people

Table 1.3 Occupational class by party choice, 1983 (%)

	Conservative	Labour	Alliance
Non-manual	63	30	59
Manual	37	70	41
	($N = 1,355$)	($N = 887$)	($N = 747$)

Source: BES data.

with different occupations voted. Table 1.3 tells us the occupational make-up of each party's voters. Thus, 44 per cent of manual workers voted Labour and manual workers constituted 70 per cent of Labour voters. Any two-variable cross-tabulation can be analysed and interpreted in two different ways like this.

Table 1.2 showed that there was a relationship between occupation and vote. We might want to ask, however, whether this relationship continues to hold when other factors are taken into account or 'controlled'. For example, we might consider whether the manual/non-manual difference still exists if we take account of the class that people *think* they belong to. We do this by constructing a three-way table. The logic of this is not difficult to understand. Having created the original two-way table with 48 cells, each cell is then divided into six (which is the number of categories into which answers to a question on self-assessed class were classified). We now have a table of no fewer than 288 cells into one of which each individual respondent can be placed. A table of this size would be very unwieldy and so, as before, cells can be omitted and combined. By doing this I have reduced the data to a table of just 18 cells, as in Table 1.4.

The table displays some complicated relationships but the basic point of Table 1.2 — that non-manual workers are more heavily Conservative and less heavily Labour than manual workers — is confirmed even when self-assessed class is taken into account.

More generally, the table illustrates two important problems with cross-tabulation analysis. Firstly, as more variables are brought into the analysis the number of cells in tables multiplies rapidly. With just three variables in the analysis we already have a basic table of 288 cells. If we were

Table 1.4 Party choice by occupational class and self-assessed class (%)

	Self-assessed 'middle'		Self-assessed 'working'		Self-assessed 'none'	
	Non-manual	Manual	Non-manual	Manual	Non-manual	Manual
Conservative	63	52	37	21	59	44
Labour	11	30	33	59	13	32
Alliance	26	19	30	21	28	24
(N)	(393)	(211)	(359)	(614)	(736)	(553)

Source: BES data.

to add another variable — age, for instance — the resulting table would be truly enormous. Tables quickly become difficult to present clearly and difficult to understand. More importantly, the number of cases within cells on which percentages are based rapidly diminishes. We started in Table 1.1 with 3,955 respondents; by Table 1.4 we are down to 2,866 and the column totals range from around 200 to 700. The addition of further variables would further reduce these.[4]

The second problem revealed by our example is that of multiple effects. While Table 1.4 shows that there are consistent differences between manual and non-manual workers, it is also the case that how people assess their class affects party choice. Manual workers who see themselves as middle class are more likely to vote Conservative than those who see themselves as working class, and so on. If we were to add a fourth variable we might find that it too had an independent effect.

The problem is how to measure and assess these different effects. There is a statistical technique for doing this, called log-linear analysis, but it is very complex and has not as yet been widely used in the literature on voting behaviour (see, however, Heath et al. 1985). Another way of coping with this difficulty is to treat nominal variables as if they were of the interval kind by assigning numeric values to the categories. This allows powerful statistical techniques which can be used with interval-scale data, in particular multiple-regression analysis (see below), to be applied to data which are essentially nominal.

Assigning numeric values is quite easy in the case of dichotomous variables. Sex, for example, could be scored 1 = female, 0 = male. When there are more than two categories things get a little more complicated. In these cases we have to create a series of dichotomous variables, one for each category, and score them as above. Thus, to convert 'party voted for' into interval form requires a variable scored 1 = voted Conservative, 0 = did not vote Conservative, then a second variable scored 1 = voted Labour, 0 = did not vote Labour and then third or fourth variables for other parties scored in the same way. The artificiality of this process is illustrated by the fact that variables created in this way are known as 'dummy' variables.

The analysis of interval-scale data

Election results yield masses of aggregate, interval-scale data. In a general election, for instance, we have the percentage turnout and the percentage share of the vote for each party in every constituency, which constitute the most obvious dependent variables in electoral analysis.

The usual starting point for analysing data of this kind is to describe the *central tendency* (or average) and *dispersion* (or spread) of a set of scores. We might want to know the average constituency turnout in the 1987 election, for example, and the extent of variation in turnout from one constituency to another. The measures most commonly employed to do this are the mean and the standard deviation, and these are explained in any introductory statistics textbook (see, for example, Startup and Whittaker 1982, Chs 2, 3).

As with nominal data, however, analysis of a single variable does not take us very far. Normally we would want to relate one or more dependent variables to other factors that might be presumed to influence them. This can be done by *correlation* and *regression* analysis. This is not as awesome as it sounds. It is not necessary for a student of voting behaviour to know how to calculate the statistics involved. Indeed, most political scientists would not know how to begin to calculate a correlation coefficient or a regression equation. Even if they did, the calculations would take hours to complete if there were a moderate number of cases involved. Nowadays, the calculations are all done by computer, and all that the student needs to know is what the results mean and the basic principles involved.

An understanding of these basic principles can be gained by starting with a piece of graph paper and a small set of data. For illustrative purposes, I will use % working class and % Labour share of the vote in 15 English constituencies in the 1987 general election.[5] The line along the bottom of the graph paper is called the *x*-axis and is used to measure the independent variable (% working class). The vertical line on the left is called the *y*-axis and is used to measure the dependent variable (% Labour). Each of the 15 constituencies can be located on the graph by checking its score on each of the two variables and plotting its position. This creates a 'scatter diagram' and Figure 1.2 shows the diagram for the 15 constituencies.

Simply by looking at the diagram we can see that there is a relationship between the two variables. As the percentage of working-class people in a constituency increases, the share of the vote obtained by Labour also tends to increase. But we can be more precise than this. Looking at the pattern in the diagram we can imagine drawing a straight line that 'best fits' the points. In fact there exists a unique straight line that does 'best fit' the data, in the sense that the sum of the distances between each point and the line is at the minimum possible.[6] The problem is to find out what this line is.

Any straight line on a graph can be described by an equation of the

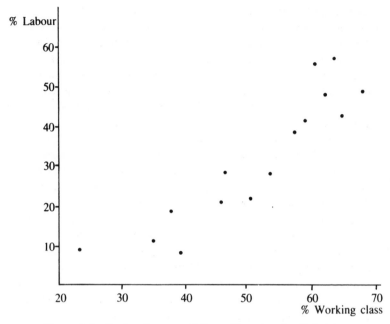

Figure 1.2 Scatter diagram of % working class by % Labour

form $y = a + b(x)$, where y is the dependent variable score, x is the independent variable score and a and b are two numbers which we do not yet know.[7] This is a regression equation. For any particular set of data the values of a and b can be calculated (very quickly by a computer) to give the equation for the best-fitting line. For the data in Figure 1.2 the equation is:

$$\% \text{ Labour} = -30.4 + 1.20(\% \text{ working class})$$

To draw the line, we simply solve the equation for two convenient scores on % working class. Thus, when % working class = 40, % Labour = 17.6 and when % working class = 70, % Labour = 53.6. If these are plotted and joined up, we have the best-fitting line.

The regression equation tells us exactly how the two variables are related. We can 'predict' the % Labour when we know the % working class just by solving the equation. 'Prediction' in this context has nothing to do with foretelling the future. It is simply that when we know a constituency's score on the independent variable we can calculate what its score on the dependent variable 'ought' to be, given the overall relationship discovered. We could, therefore, identify deviant cases, where the Labour vote is noticeably higher or lower than it 'ought' to be.

Knowing how two variables are related is important but it is only half of the story. We also need to know how strongly they are related. The same regression line could be the best fit of a series of points that were well spread out around the line or of another series closely clustered around it. In the latter case the relationship would be a stronger one. The strength of a relationship is measured by a statistic called the *correlation coefficient* (properly the Pearson product−moment correlation coefficient), which is signified as *r*. The value of *r* varies from +1 through 0 to −1. Where it is positive, this indicates (unsurprisingly) that the two variables are positively related. This means that as the independent variable increases so does the dependent variable. Where *r* is negative, this means that as the independent variable increases the dependent variable decreases. The regression line will then slope down from left to right. If I had used % Conservative as the dependent variable in the above example that is what would have resulted.

The closer *r* is to +1 or −1, the stronger the relationship is; the closer to 0 it is, the weaker the relationship. Values of +1 or −1 indicate absolutely perfect correlations. In that case all the points in a scatter diagram would be exactly on the regression line, and if we knew the independent variable score we could calculate with complete accuracy the dependent variable score. Conversely, a correlation of 0 would mean that there was no (linear) relationship whatsoever between the two variables.

In practice, correlations of 1 or 0 are unheard of in electoral analysis. The illustration above produced a correlation coefficient of 0.90, which indicates a very strong relationship. (This is not a surprise since the 15 constituencies were specifically selected to demonstrate a clear relationship.) For the same constituencies, the correlation between % Conservative and % working class is −0.86 (a strong negative correlation), and when % Alliance is the dependent variable the coefficient is −0.32 (which is, given the small number of cases involved, a weak negative correlation).

I briefly noted above that we can measure the extent to which scores on variables are dispersed or concentrated by calculating the standard deviation. The square of the standard deviation (the standard deviation multiplied by itself) is called the *variance* and this is a measure of the total amount of variation in a set of data. An important feature of the correlation coefficient is that if it too is squared, then the resulting figure (r^2) is the proportion of the variation in the dependent variable that is statistically 'explained' or 'accounted for' by variations in the scores on the independent variable. Proportions are slightly cumbersome to handle and so they are normally converted to percentages by moving the decimal point two places to the right. Thus, the correlation between % working class and % Labour in our 15 constituencies is 0.90, so $r^2 = 0.810$; that is, 81.0 per cent of the variation in the Labour vote in these seats is accounted for by variations in the size of the working class from one constituency to another. Similarly, variations in the % working class account for 74.0 per cent of the variation in the Conservative vote and for only 10.2 per cent of the variation in the Alliance vote.

This brief outline has attempted to explain in a simple way the principles underlying correlation and regression analysis and, although it is difficult to illustrate it visually, the same principles can be extended to analysis using two or more independent variables. This *multivariate* analysis enables numerous factors to be taken into account simultaneously by the use of what is called *multiple regression*. For example, to return to the 15 constituencies I have used for illustration, we could add another independent variable to the analysis, say % owner-occupiers. We now know two things about each constituency in addition to the distribution of the vote. Does this improve our ability to account for variations in party support? As before, we can calculate regression equations and their associated r^2 statistics. In this case, with % Labour as the dependent variable the equation is:

$$\% \text{ Labour } = -46.1 + 1.34(\% \text{ working class}) \\ + 0.16(\% \text{ owner-occupiers})$$

The multiple r^2 is 0.830 so that 83 per cent of the variation in the Labour vote is accounted for by the two independent variables. Adding % owner-occupiers has increased our ability to predict the Labour vote by two percentage points. In principle, as many variables as desired can be added, but many will be found not to make any difference to the r^2 and can be discarded as not adding to the explanatory power of the equations. Much electoral analysis of this kind involves a search for a high r^2, which is frequently taken as a sign of analytical success.

Interpreting correlation coefficients

Correlation analysis is relatively easy to do (on a computer). Once the data are in a suitable form, it is simply a matter of punching them into the computer and calling up an appropriate programme. Correlation coefficients will then be churned out by the hundred in a few seconds. But care must be taken in interpreting these statistics which are very frequently used in the literature on elections. Four important points should be borne in mind.

Firstly, correlation does not equal causation. Just because two variables are strongly associated it does not follow that one *causes* the other. Correlation tells us just what it says — the extent to which variables co-relate — nothing more and nothing less. Secondly, an associated point, for a correlation to be of interest it must be of some theoretical significance. For all I know, there may be a strong correlation between the percentage of people in a consistuency who have red hair and the size of the Alliance vote. But such a relationship would be virtually meaningless because there is no theory, hypothesis or suggestion as to why hair colour and party choice should be connected. The world is full of 'spurious' correlations, that is, phenomena which are statistically related but have absolutely no other conceivable connection. Thirdly, correlations based on aggregate data tell us nothing about the behaviour of individuals. The fact that there is a strong positive correlation between the percentage of working-class people in a constituency and the percentage of the vote obtained by Labour *cannot* be used to infer that working-class people vote Labour. Although there may be a presumption that this is the case, all that can properly be inferred from the correlation is that the more working-class people there are the higher is the Labour vote. We can draw conclusions about collectivities, constituencies, not the individuals who comprise them.[8] This distinction is very important. Inferring individual behaviour from aggregate statistics is known as the 'ecological fallacy' and is one of the most grievous sins an electoral analyst can commit. Fourthly, the absence of a high correlation coefficient does not mean that two variables are completely unrelated. Most correlation and regression analysis is concerned with linear (straight-line) relationships but it is possible that variables may be related in other (curvilinear) ways. Without more advanced statistical techniques, the only way to check for non-linear patterns is by visual inspection of scatter diagrams.

Measuring electoral change

Thus far I have discussed the analysis of the results of a single election. This is sometimes called 'cross-sectional' analysis. But, of course, elections are held regularly in Britain — once at least every five years in the case of general elections and more frequently in the case of local elections. When a series of elections is brought into consideration, we immediately have a new set of dependent variables, namely, *changes* in turnout and in the distribution of votes from one election to another. In order to summarise changes in party support psephologists have made much use of a measure known as 'swing'.

Swing was developed by Dr David Butler. It is simple to calculate and is defined as follows:

$$\frac{(C2-C1) + (L1-L2)}{2}$$

In this formula, C1 is the percentage share of the total vote obtained by the Conservatives at the first election and C2 the percentage at the second; L1 is Labour's share at the first election and L2 Labour's percentage at the second. The statistic produced by this formula is known as 'Butler' or 'traditional' swing. By convention the parties are put in the order shown and the effect of this is that a positive figure denotes a swing to the Conservatives and a negative figure a swing to Labour. But the parties could appear in any order and any two parties could be substituted for Conservative and Labour.

A variant known as 'two-party' or 'Steed' swing (having been devised by Michael Steed) is also commonly used. Here the formula is exactly as above but, when calculating the percentage vote for the two parties concerned, votes for all other parties are excluded, so that the two parties' shares of the vote always total 100 per cent.

In the past, swing was a widely used and very useful measure of electoral change. It provided a simple summary of the extent of change and was used to compare inter-election movements in different parts of the country and different constituencies. In addition, before general elections psephologists could work out the swing needed for any constituency to change hands. Thus, if a constituency had voted 54 per cent Conservative and 46 per cent Labour at the preceding election, then a swing to Labour of anything over 4 per cent would mean a Labour gain. Since swing tended to be in the same direction and of the same magnitude over the country as a whole, accurate estimates could be made of the number of seats that would change hands given a particular national swing and of the swing needed for a party to win or lose a majority of seats in the House of Commons.

These properties of swing enabled it to become the only statistical idea I know of which made someone a television personality. In the days before computer graphics, the late Robert McKenzie used to appear regularly on TV election programmes with a simple pendulum device which he called a 'swingometer'. When he moved it the appropriate number of points each way, it would show which seats were likely to change hands. The 'swingometer' was creaky but it was effective and certainly did a lot to educate the general public about the operation of elections and the electoral system in Britain.

The problem is that swing works well only if elections are essentially contests between two parties. As Britain has moved to a situation in which patterns of party competition are much more complex, swing has lost its usefulness (see McAllister and Rose 1984, Ch. 9). There have been attempts to devise three-way swing figures but these are complicated to work out and lack the elegance and simplicity of traditional swing. The commonest way of measuring aggregate or net electoral change nowadays is simply to calculate the changes in each party's percentage share of the vote.

These, like swing, are summary statistics. They do not tell us anything about how individuals behave but rather describe the net effect of the changes in individuals' voting behaviour between two elections. This can be easily understood if we separate the different components of electoral change.

Whether over the country as a whole or in individual constituencies or wards (assuming no boundary changes), the differences between two consecutive election results are produced by four factors:

(1)   Switching between major parties. (For simplicity, I shall treat the Conservatives and Labour as the major parties). Some people who voted Labour in the first election will vote Conservative in the second and *vice versa*. Clearly the outcome of the second election will be affected only if there is some imbalance in these switches.

(2)   Minor-party traffic. Here again party switching is involved but this time from minor parties (such as the Democrats, Greens and SNP) to one of the major parties and also to minor parties from one of the major parties. (There may also be some movement between different minor parties.) As with (1) there will be some self-cancelling effect but an imbalance will affect the election outcome.

(3)   Non-voting traffic. Not everyone votes in every election. Some people who did not vote in the first election will vote in the second; others who voted first time round fail to do so the second time. Clearly, if one party's previous supporters stay away from the polls in larger numbers

or if previous non-voters flock to one particular party this will affect the result.

(4) The physical replacement of the electorate. Every year (although the number fluctuates a little) around 750,000 people in Britain become 18, and therefore eligible to vote, while about 650,000 people die. If one party gets a disproportionate share of the new voters, or if the supporters of one party are dying off in greater numbers, this will affect election outcomes. Immigration to and emigration from the country or a particular constituency can have a similar effect. It is not unusual for population movement to change completely the character of a ward or constituency over time.

Aggregate measures of electoral change, such as swing, simply summarise the effects of all of these ebbs and flows. For more detailed information about the various components of change we have to turn to individual-level data produced by surveys.

Ideally, a survey study designed to analyse electoral change would interview a sample of voters after one election and then reinterview the same 'panel' after a second election. This minimises the chance of respondents mis-remembering how they voted in a previous election which may have been held as many as five years before. It is, of course, not possible to reinterview people who have died between the two elections and it is difficult to identify respondents who are too young to vote in the first election but reach voting age by the time of the second.

None the less, when a survey obtains the reported votes of respondents at two successive elections the components of electoral change can be investigated by constructing a two-way table showing exactly what people did at the two elections. A table of this kind is sometimes called an 'election transition matrix' or, more simply, a 'flow of the vote' table and Table 1.5 is an example.[9]

Between the elections of 1983 and 1987 the election results show that, overall, the changes in the parties' shares of the votes were Conservative −0.1 per cent, Labour +3.2 per cent and Alliance −2.8 per cent. These figures suggest a high degree of stability. By considering the survey evidence in Table 1.5, however, we can see that this net result was a product of considerable movement among voters — much of it self-cancelling. Thus, 5 per cent of 1983 Conservatives switched to Labour and 12 per cent switched to the Alliance, but this was almost balanced by the fact that 4 per cent of 1983 Labour voters and 10 per cent of 1983 Alliance voters switched to the Conservatives.

Table 1.5 Flow of the vote, 1983−87 (%)

	Vote in 1983				
	Con.	Lab.	Alliance	Non-voter	Too young
Vote in 1987					
Con.	77	4	10	21	28
Lab.	5	75	12	19	24
Alliance	12	11	70	14	14
Other	—	1	1	1	1
Non-voter	6	8	8	45	32

Source: Crewe (1987a).
Notes: These data are derived from a Gallup survey of 4,886 electors commissioned by BBC Television. The table is not a complete transition matrix since it excludes 'other' party voters in 1983 as well as those who died between elections.

Clearly, then, aggregate measures of change between elections, while important and necessary, are limited. A fuller understanding of electoral change requires the kind of detailed information about individuals that only surveys can provide.[10]

Aggregate and survey data compared

Aggregate and survey data are both extensively used in electoral analysis and both have advantages and drawbacks. The advantages of using aggregate data are as follows:

(1) If it is confined to publicly available data it is cheap. It costs thousands of pounds to employ a firm to undertake a national survey of the British electorate. Even a modest local survey is expensive. In contrast, anyone can go to a library and collect election results, census data and the like and then, armed only with a small calculator and a knowledge of some elementary statistical techniques, embark upon analysis.

(2) Aggregate data such as election results reflect real behaviour, what voters actually did, while surveys report what voters *say* they have done. There is sometimes a disjunction between these. Surveys always find, for instance, that more people claim to have voted in an election than actually did, according to the election returns.

(3)   Aggregate data usually refer to the total population being studied and are, therefore, not susceptible to sampling error in the way that survey data are.

(4)   Aggregate data are almost always interval-scale data and are suitable for analysing with the most powerful statistical techniques.

(5)   Survey studies of electoral behaviour are of relatively recent origin whereas masses of relevant aggregate data — in particular election results — are available going back to the nineteenth century.

On the other hand, surveys also have important advantages:

(1)   Whereas with aggregate data we are usually restricted to material that has been collected and published — there are, for example, no official figures showing the distribution of different religions in British constituencies — in surveys the investigator can ask for any information that seems appropriate.

(2)   More precisely, aggregate statistics refer only to the objective characteristics and behaviour of a population. It is only by using surveys that the beliefs, attitudes and opinions of voters can be discovered.

(3)   Most important of all, however, individual data collected by survey permit analysis of individuals rather than collectivities. I have already commented on the importance of this with respect to electoral change, but it is of more general significance in electoral analysis. Without surveys we would not know which groups vote for which parties and in what proportions, and our theories about why people vote the way they do would be highly speculative.

My purpose in this chapter has not been to provide a comprehensive introduction to statistics. Rather it has been to familiarise those who know little about such matters with some of the statistical terms, measures and techniques which proliferate in the elections literature. I hope that the chapter has made this literature more accessible to the non-specialist and has provided a foundation for understanding the substantive material considered in subsequent chapters.

Notes

1.   There is a third scale of measurement — the ordinal scale — which I have ignored. Ordinal data are rarely analysed differently from the other two kinds.

2. Almost all elementary textbooks on statistics in social science do this. See, for example, Startup and Whittaker (1982).

3. 'Exit' polls involve interviewing voters as they leave the polling station after having voted.

4. Dunleavy and Husbands (1985, p. 133) have a table showing vote by trade union membership, gender and social class in which percentages are based on numbers ranging from 14 to 77.

5. The constituencies are Barnsley West and Penistone, Basildon, Bethnal Green and Stepney, Chichester, Darlington, Epping Forest, Esher, Gloucester, Guildford, Makerfield, Milton Keynes, Nottingham East, Pudsey. The figures for % working class are taken from Butler and Kavanagh (1988).

6. Technically it is the sum of the *squares* of the distance that is set at a minimum and the line is known as the 'least squares' line.

7. Anyone who doubts that this equation inevitably produces a straight line can check it very simply. Assign any values at all to a and b and then calculate the value of y for different values of x. For example, if $a = 2$ and $b = 4$ then when $x = 1$, $y = 2+4(1) = 6$; when $x = 2$, $y = 2+4(2) = 10$, and so on. If the x and y values are plotted against one another it will be found that they fall in a straight line.

8. In this example, for instance, it might be the case that in all constituencies a similar minority of working-class people vote Labour, but as the % working class increases a larger proportion of *middle-class* people vote Labour. This would have the effect of producing a positive correlation between % working class and % Labour.

9. Fuller examples of election transition matrices, including estimates of the population entering and leaving the electorate, are given in Butler and Stokes (1974, Ch. 12) and Sarlvik and Crewe (1983, Ch. 2).

10. Details of the different components of swing for each pair of elections between 1959 and 1979 can be found in Crewe (1985a, p. 113).

2

The Era of Alignment, 1950 – 70

The British general election of 1945 took place in very unusual circumstances. It was the first general election for 10 years, the country was still at war with Japan and very many voters were serving in the Forces overseas (almost three million electors were registered as service voters). Given these circumstances, the best starting point for a review of post-war elections and electoral behaviour is not 1945 but 1950, the year of the first 'normal' post-war general election.

In this chapter, I consider the results of survey studies of voting between 1950 and 1970 and suggest that this period can be characterised as one of 'aligned' voting. First, however, it is necessary to look briefly at early American work in the field, since this had a major impact on voting research in Britain.

Two models of voting behaviour

Survey-based studies of voting behaviour in Britain in the 1950s and 1960s — and right up to today — have been very much influenced by theories, models and methods developed in the United States. Two major approaches have been influential.

The first, which might be called the 'social determinism' approach, emphasised the way in which party choice appeared to be an almost automatic consequence of a voter's social characteristics. The authors of the first-ever survey study of American voting behaviour, *The People's Choice* (Lazarsfeld et al. 1968), had intended to focus upon short-term factors affecting voting choice in the presidential election of 1940 — the book was subtitled 'How the voter makes up his mind in a presidential campaign' — but they became more impressed by the importance of social characteristics such as class and religion. They concluded (p. 27) that 'a person thinks, politically, as he is socially. Social characteristics determine political preference.' Lazarsfeld and his colleagues discovered that they could predict a person's vote with considerable accuracy from knowledge of just a few social characteristics.

Describing relationships between various social and demographic characteristics and party choice — while always interesting — is not, however, in itself very useful. It would certainly be interesting if it were found that left-handed people with brown eyes tended to vote in a distinctive way but it seems unlikely that knowing this will advance our understanding of what motivates voters. What is required is some theory that explains why there should be a link between specific social characteristics and voting. We need an answer to the question: Why should some social differences be associated with political differences whereas others are not?

In 1948 the authors of *The People's Choice* carried out a second study and in *Voting* (Berelson et al. 1954) they extended and reinforced their original argument. In particular, they provided an answer to the above question by suggesting that for a social difference to be translated into a political cleavage three conditions need to be fulfilled. These are:

(1) initial social differentiation such that the consequences of political policy are materially or symbolically different for different groups; (2) conditions of transmittibility from generation to generation; and (3) conditions of physical and social proximity providing for continued in-group contact in succeeding generations (p. 75).

The first condition requires that the social groups concerned must have differing material or symbolic interests which are affected by government policy. Thus council tenants and owner-occupiers might have different interests with regard to housing policy. Policy in areas like abortion or embryo research might not directly affect many people but could be said to be of symbolic importance to some groups such as Roman Catholics and others. On the other hand, 'groups' such as the left-handed or the red-headed are not normally treated differently from the rest of the population in matters of public policy and do not fulfil the first condition. The second and third conditions relate to the processes by which social and political divisions are maintained and reinforced.

We have here, then, what might be termed an 'interests plus socialisation' theory or model. Different social groups have different interests and hence different needs. They therefore tend to vote for different parties which they perceive as representing these interests. Awareness of a group's distinctiveness and of group—party links is sustained by regular contact with fellow group members in the family, among peers and in the community.

This is an appealing and apparently simple model but it is not without difficulties. Very briefly, four problems with the model are as follows:

(1) Overlapping group memberships. Everyone belongs to a variety of social groups and the theory offers no clues as to which will be decisive in determining an individual's party support, and why.

(2) Group interests. It is not self-evident that a large and relatively heterogeneous group of people will have the same interests. Who decides what the group's interests are, and in what sense can political parties be said to represent group interests?

(3) Deviants. How does the model account for the (often large) minorities who do not conform to group voting norms?

(4) Political parties. The theory tends to give the impression that party choice is a sort of spontaneous effect of social location and ignores the active role that political parties play in mobilising and structuring the electorate.

Despite criticisms of this kind, some form of 'social determinism' underpinned by the idea of 'interests plus socialisation' has heavily influenced voting research in Britain.

The second major American influence on British voting studies derives from a book called *The American Voter* (Campbell et al. 1960). In this profoundly influential study Campbell and his colleagues developed a model of voting behaviour which has come to be known as the 'Michigan model', since the original research was directed from the University of Michigan. Like the 'social determinism' model, the Michigan model suggests that long-term factors are most important in determining party choice. But there is not a simple step from social location to voting behaviour. Rather, the social position that an individual occupies affects the kinds of influence that he or she will encounter in interacting with family, friends, neighbours, workmates and so on. As a consequence of these interactions — especially within the family — the individual acquires a *party identification*. This means a sense of attachment to a party, a feeling of commitment to it, being a supporter of the party — rather like being an Everton supporter or a Wimbledon supporter — and not just someone who happens to vote for the party from time to time.

When there is an election, there is an interaction between a voter's long-term party identification and various short-term influences, such as current political issues, campaign events, the personalities of party leaders or candidates and, we might add, the tactical situation in the local constituency, to produce a vote decision. The Michigan team were at pains to emphasise, however, that it is the long-term factors that are usually decisive. Indeed a person's party identification will influence how he or she interprets and evaluates issues, party leaders and so on.

The concept of party identification is central to the Michigan model and it is worth exploring it in a little more detail. It is important to grasp that identifying with a party is not the same as voting for it. Indeed it is possible to identify with one party and vote for a different one. This happens frequently in American presidential elections. President Reagan's electoral success was largely due to his ability to get Democratic party identifiers to vote for him, even although he was a Republican. But the same sort of thing happens in Britain. A Labour supporter living in a constituency in which Labour has no realistic chance of winning — Chelmsford for example — might decide to vote Democrat while still remaining basically a Labour supporter.

There are three clear differences between party identification and voting. Firstly, party identification is psychological while voting is behavioural. That is, identification exists in people's heads; we cannot observe it directly. Voting, however, is a definite action — putting a cross on a piece of paper or pulling a lever on a voting machine — and it is, in principle, observable (although normally done in secret). Secondly, voting is time-specific while party identification is not. Voting can take place only at an election — and elections occur relatively infrequently in Britain — whereas identification is ongoing and continuous. There does not need to be an election in the offing for people to consider themselves supporters of a party. Thirdly, party identification varies in intensity and voting does not. Some people will be very strong party supporters, others not very strong or just weak supporters. All votes count equally, however, whether the voter marks the ballot with a great thick black cross or a tiny faint one.

Party identification is, then, distinct from voting. This means that it can be used to help explain party choice in an election, as in the Michigan model. According to the theory, party identification serves important functions for the individual. It simplifies the task of understanding the complex world of politics. Once someone decides (or has learned) who are the 'goodies' and who the 'baddies' there is no need to pay great attention to the details of political debate, no need to bother with the details of party policies or election manifestos. Identification also acts as a sort of psychological filter or prism through which political messages pass to the individual; it provides a framework within which political events are understood and evaluated.

When party identification is widespread, it has important effects on the political system as a whole. Most obviously it provides an element of stability and continuity. (Everton supporters do not suddenly switch their affections to Liverpool or Manchester United, and it is much the same with political parties.) If people identify with a party they are not likely to shoot off in all directions at successive elections. Rather, they will have a 'normal' vote which in most cases will remain stable from election to election.

Aligned voting in Britain, 1950–70

When these approaches were applied to Britain in the 1950s and 1960s, a clear picture of the British electorate emerged. This is summarised in Figure 2.1. Broadly speaking, the electorate was divided into two great blocs which provided reliable and stable voting support for the Conservative and Labour parties. The interconnected phenomena of class and partisan alignment were the twin pillars, as it were, which supported

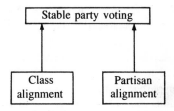

Figure 2.1   Aligned voting in Britain

and sustained stable party support on the part of individual voters and a stable two-party system overall.

Partisan alignment

By partisan alignment I mean a situation in which voters align themselves with a party by thinking of themselves as supporters of it, by having a party identification. This was certainly the case in Britain in the 1950s and 1960s. The standard survey question designed to elicit the kind of generalised psychological commitment implied by party identification is: 'Generally speaking do you think of yourself as Conservative, Labour, Liberal or what?' Surveys at the three elections between 1964 and 1970 found that the overwhelming majority of voters were willing to nominate a party that they supported, and of those most nominated the Labour or Conservative parties (see Table 2.1).

It is possible that the survey question normally used does not in fact tap the kind of enduring, deep-rooted commitment which is implied by the concept of party identification, but that voters respond by simply naming the party they currently favour. This possibility has been considered by, among others, Butler and Stokes (1974, pp. 39–47) and Crewe, Sarlvik and Alt (1977, pp. 139–42). Both studies showed that voters were more likely to change votes without changing identification and concluded that this shows that the question 'works' and that party identification really did exist amongst voters. As Butler and Stokes put it, 'it is clear that millions of British electors remain anchored to one of the parties for very long periods of time. Indeed many electors have had the same party loyalties from the dawn of their political consciousness' (p. 47). Common experience confirms that party identification exists.

Table 2.1 Party identification, 1964–70 (%)

	1964	1966	1970
With party identification	92	90	89
With Conservative or Labour identification	81	80	81
'Very strong' identifiers	43	43	41
'Very strong' Conservative or Labour	40	39	40

Source: Sarlvik and Crewe (1983, pp. 334–5).

We all know people who are 'Conservatives' or 'Labour supporters' rather than people who just happen to vote Conservative or Labour at a specific election.

As a standard follow-up to the party identification question in election surveys, respondents are asked how strongly Conservative or Labour or whatever they feel. People can be characterised as 'very strong' identifiers, 'fairly strong' or 'not very strong'. In the three surveys reported in Table 2.1, more than two-fifths of the electorate were prepared to describe themselves as 'very strong' party supporters and almost all of these were Conservative or Labour identifiers.

Strength of party identification has important effects upon electoral behaviour. Stronger identifiers are more likely to turn out to vote, to vote for the party they identify with, and to be stable in their party choice over time than are weaker identifiers. The latter are more likely to make their minds up about who to vote for closer to election day itself, rather than well in advance of it, and to be more 'wobbly' in the sense of seriously considering voting for a party other than their eventual choice. I shall return to these important differences in later chapters.

Clearly, then, a partisan alignment existed in Britain during this period. The extent and strength of commitment to the Conservative and Labour parties provided a basis for stability in electoral behaviour and for a two-party system that seemed secure.

Class alignment

Between 1950 and 1970, of all the possible social characteristics that might have influenced party choice, social class was consistently found to be the most important. Generally, about two-thirds of working-class voters supported the Labour party and upwards of four-fifths of the middle class voted Conservative. Writing in 1967, Peter Pulzer concluded, in a much-quoted sentence, that 'Class is the basis of British party politics; all else is embellishment and detail' (1967, p. 98). Similarly, on the basis of figures such as those given in Table 2.2, Butler and Stokes reported:

> Our findings on the strength of links between class and partisanship in Britain echo broadly those of every other opinion poll or voting study ... there were strong enough cross-currents in each class for partisanship not to have been determined entirely by class. Yet its pre-eminent role can hardly be questioned (1974, p. 77).

There was, then, an alignment between class and party. Britain was, indeed, considered the archetypal class-based party system. Before

Table 2.2 Party self-image by occupational status, 1963 (%)

	Higher managerial	Lower managerial	Supervisory non-manual	Lower non-manual	Skilled manual	Unskilled manual
Conservative	87	81	77	61	29	25
Labour	14	19	23	39	71	75

Source: Butler and Stokes (1974, p. 78).
Note: The table is restricted to respondents with a Conservative or Labour 'self-image', which is the term used by Butler and Stokes to denote identification.

accepting this, however, we need to pause for a moment to consider what exactly 'social class' is.

Defining class

Despite its central position in voting behaviour research, the concept of class is slippery and difficult to define precisely. It is even more difficult to measure or 'operationalise' in empirical research.

When we say that a person is 'middle class' or 'working class' we often have a variety of things in mind — wealth, income, occupation, education, accent, 'style of life' and so on. So how is a person's class to be determined? Generally, voting researchers, as well as opinion pollsters and market researchers, have opted for occupation as a shorthand indicator of class. This can be justified on the grounds that most people describe different classes in terms of different occupations (see Butler and Stokes 1974, p. 70) but it also gives rise to other problems. How many classes are there? Which occupations belong to which classes? The classes of bank managers and coal miners may be fairly obvious, but what about typists, policemen or foremen on building sites? Is a self-employed plumber in a different class from a plumber who is employed by a large firm?

Another set of problems relates to the categorisation of women. Should employed married women be classified according to their own job or the job of their husbands (the reasoning being that the husband is the 'head of the household' and thus determines the whole family's status)? And what about married women who are full-time housewives and mothers?

Clearly, the definition and measurement of this most basic social variable is fraught with difficulty. Indeed, as we shall see in Chapter

3, the very definition of class has come to be an important element in the current debate about the level of class voting in Britain.

Opinion polling firms have developed comprehensive schemes for coding (or classifying) occupations into five main groups whose names have become familiar to poll-watchers. These are:

A   Higher professional, managerial and administrative.
B   Intermediate professional, managerial and administrative.
C1   Supervisory, clerical and other non-manual.
C2   Skilled manual.
D   Semi-skilled and unskilled manual.
E   Residual, casual workers, people reliant on state benefits.

Voting researchers, however, have usually combined these into two groups — non-manual workers (ABC1) and manual workers (C2DE). This is partly for purely practical reasons. If a survey uses a five-fold categorisation, the number of respondents in each class will be smaller than with a dichotomous scheme and detailed analysis will be inhibited. Partly also the reality is that most people do seem to think of the British class structure in terms of a basic division between a middle and a working class. Nevertheless, it should be borne in mind that the manual/non-manual distinction is a very rough-and-ready approximation to what we mean when we talk about social class.

Other social influences on voting

Although class was the dominant source of political alignment in Britain in the 1950s and 1960s, other social and demographic characteristics were also consistently found to be associated with party choice. Two preliminary points about these relationships should be noted. Firstly, the importance of class as a determinant of voting was such that for any other variable to be shown to have an effect it had to have such an effect when class was 'controlled' (see Chapter 1). There would, for example, be little point in getting excited over a finding that most Roman Catholics voted Labour if it were also the case that most Roman Catholics were working class. Secondly, while the job of establishing the existence of positive relationships between social attributes and party choice is relatively straightforward, explaining them is not. Voting researchers might agree about which groups vote for which parties but that does not mean that they are in agreement about why they do so.

Table 2.3 Conservative lead over Labour by age and class, 1970

	Age				
	18–24	*25–34*	*35–49*	*50–64*	*65+*
Upper-middle class	10	25	49	63	66
Lower-middle class	−9	17	20	37	28
Working class	−19	−16	−17	−12	−3

Source: Rose (1974, p. 521).
Note: The figure in each cell is % Conservative minus % Labour among the class/age
    group concerned.

Age

There is a well-known aphorism, the origins of which are obscure, which
goes something like this: 'If you're not a radical at 20 you've no heart;
if you're not a conservative at 60 you've no head.' The precise ages
referred to vary a lot but the general sentiment of this piece of folk-
wisdom is clear enough and it appeared to find some empirical support
from voting studies in the 1950s and 1960s. Academic surveys and opinion polls regularly found that younger people, especially the youngest
age group in the electorate, were more inclined to vote Labour while
older voters favoured the Conservatives.

A typical set of figures, reported by Richard Rose for the 1970 general
election, is given in Table 2.3. Rose controlled for the effect of class
by using a three-fold classification of occupations (splitting non-manual
workers into an 'upper-middle' class — the A and B groups — and a
'lower-middle' class — the C1 group). It is clear that within each class
there is an age effect. As we move up the age groups the Conservative
lead over Labour increases or Labour's lead decreases. What is not clear
is why this should be so.

Two main explanations have been offered. The first suggests what is
called a 'life-cycle' effect and is essentially the explanation implicit in
the aphorism quoted above. Young people tend to be idealistic and to
favour social and political change. As they grow older, however, people acquire more responsibilities, more of a stake in society (such as
property) and become more aware of the difficulties associated with rapid
social change. They thus become more cautious and conservative in
outlook.

The second explanation concentrates on political generations or
'cohorts'. In this view, it is not so much a person's age that is important

as when he or she was young and beginning to experience politics. As each generation enters the electorate it is influenced by currently decisive political events — the Vietnam War in the 1960s, for example, or the 'winter of discontent' in 1978/9 — or, more broadly, 'the nature of the times'. Thus, people voting for the first time in 1945 would have been influenced by having lived through a war and the strongly pro-Labour feeling in the country at that time. Their political attitudes and behaviour would continue to be influenced by this for a long time. Using the idea of political generations, the strength of Conservative support among older people in Britain in the 1950s and 1960s could be explained by the fact that anyone aged over 60 in, say, 1964 would have come of age in the 1920s or before, when Labour was a relatively new party. Their earliest influences, therefore, were unlikely to have been in a pro-Labour direction.

As in so many cases, there is something to be said for both of these views. Generally, however, the data — including data from other countries in which increasing age is also associated with increasing conservatism — are more supportive of the 'life-cycle' rather than the generational approach. The tendency for Labour support to be weaker among older age groups persists as different generations move through the electorate.

Sex

Like age, a person's sex is not usually too difficult to discover and classify.[1] In this case too, in the 1950s and 1960s there was a regular pattern: men were less likely to vote Conservative and more likely to vote Labour than women. As Pulzer put it:

> There is overwhelming evidence that women are more Conservatively inclined than men ... sex is the one factor which indubitably counter-balances class trends: working-class women are more right-wing than working-class men, middle-class women are more right-wing than middle-class men (1967, p. 107).

Table 2.4, which is again taken from Rose, illustrates this. By controlling for class, the possibility that women are more Conservative because they are more likely to have non-manual occupations is excluded. What is not excluded, however, is the possibility that the apparent sex difference is actually an age difference, since women live longer than men. There is, however, no shortage of other hypotheses to explain the

Table 2.4 Conservative lead over Labour by sex and
class, 1970

	Sex	
	Male	*Female*
Upper-middle class	47	50
Lower-middle class	13	20
Working class	−21	−7

Source: Rose (1974, p. 522)
Note: The figure in each cell is % Conservative minus %
Labour among the class/sex group concerned.

greater Conservatism of women. It can be argued, for instance, that
women in working-class families have traditionally been more home-
centred than men. While men went out to work women stayed at home
to look after children. This insulated them from industrial conflicts and
wider community pressures. Women may also be the bearers of
traditional values, relating to religion and the family for example,
and thus are more Conservative. It has even been suggested that women
are more socially aspiring than men, which is why they also have more
'genteel', less strongly regional accents.[2]

Religion

The following incident is recorded in Butler and Stokes' discussion of
religion and voting:

> One of our interviewers recorded a colloquy with a respondent who said
> 'none' in answer to her initial question about religious affiliation. She then
> inquired, on her own initiative, whether she ought to put him down as
> 'atheist' or 'agnostic'. The respondent thereupon asked to be told the dif-
> ference between the two ... After hearing her account, the respondent
> said, 'You had better put me down as Church of England' (1974, pp.
> 156–7).

This illustrates very well the difficulty of classifying voters according
to religious denomination and of analysing the relationship between
religion and party choice. The respondent presumably *was* put down as
C. of E. and incorporated into the analysis on that basis. In a largely
secular, non-churchgoing society it is not clear what it means to say that
someone 'belongs' to one religion or another.

None the less, in many western European states religion remains a highly important determinant of party choice. And the same was true of Britain in the late nineteenth and early twentieth centuries. In those days, the Church of England could fairly be described as 'the Tory party at prayer' while the Liberal party was strongly supported by Nonconformists. Religious issues, such as support for Established Church schools from the rates (local taxes) or the question of the disestablishment of the Anglican Church in Wales, excited much political passion.[3]

By the 1950s and 1960s, however, the influence of religion on political party choice, although still in evidence (and of paramount importance in Northern Ireland), had greatly declined. Table 2.5 shows that middle-class Anglicans were more likely to support the Conservative party than were Nonconformists or Roman Catholics, and that working-class Nonconformists and Roman Catholics were more strongly Labour. The relatively strong support for the Liberals among middle-class Nonconformists is also clear. Butler and Stokes, from whom this table is taken, do not give figures for people who have no religious affilation but other evidence shows that this group was inclined to support Labour (for a fuller discussion see Bochel and Denver 1970).

Explanations for the association between religion and party have tended to focus on the fact that the Church of England, as the Established Church, is identified with the social and political establishment, while religious dissent goes hand in hand with political dissent. Catholics in Britain are to a considerable extent descendants of Irish immigrants, and for them the Conservatives are identified as the party which vigorously opposed Irish Home Rule and supported Ulster Protestants in forcing the partition of Ireland in 1922.

As this point illustrates, the influence of religion on party choice in

Table 2.5 Party self-image by religion and class, 1963 (%)

	Middle class				Working class			
	C. of E.	C. of Scot.	Non-conformist	R.C.	C. of E.	C. of Scot.	Non-conformist	R.C.
Con.	72	74	41	55	30	25	22	18
Lab.	10	22	22	26	55	59	62	68
Lib.	18	4	37	19	15	16	16	14

Source: Butler and Stokes (1974, p. 158).

the 1950s and 1960s was very much a legacy of past struggles. Butler and Stokes were convinced that it was a legacy that was steadily disappearing. Only in Northern Ireland itself, and in parts of mainland Britain where the Irish influence remained strong, did religion continue to have a powerful impact on party choice.

Region and locality

In analysing regional voting patterns, students of elections have generally made use of the 'standard regions' defined by the Registrar-General's Office for census and other purposes. In this definition, England is divided into eight regions — the North, Yorkshire and Humberside, East Midlands, East Anglia, South East, South West, West Midlands, and the North West — while Scotland, Wales and Northern Ireland are also defined as standard regions. Dividing up the country in this way is inevitably rather arbitrary and it is unlikely that everyone living in these regions feels a distinctive regional identity (excepting, of course, Scotland, Wales and Northern Ireland, where people would resent the use of the term 'region'). People living in Newcastle upon Tyne, for example, would consider themselves 'Geordies' rather than inhabitants of the North region.

None the less, despite the artificiality of official regional boundaries, elections in the 1950s and 1960s were marked by very clear regional voting patterns which were reproduced in election after election. Indeed, Rose (1974, p. 490) demonstrates that these regional patterns stretch right back to 1918 with very little alteration. Very broadly, Britain was divided into 'two nations' electorally. Labour support was higher and Conservative support lower in Scotland, Wales and northern England[4] than in the rest of England.

To some extent, this pattern reflects differences in the social composition of the electorate. Since there were (and are) more working-class people in Scotland, Wales and the North than elsewhere, Labour would be expected to do better anyway. But even when class is controlled, regional differences persist. Table 2.6 shows how people of different classes voted in the mid-1960s within two broad regional groupings. As can be seen, within both classes the Conservative share of the vote is larger and Labour's smaller in the South and Midlands.

This table is restricted to Conservative and Labour voters only, and it gives no information about two other distinctively regional features of elections during this period. The first was the distribution of support

Table 2.6   Party support by region and class, 1963−6 (%)

	Scotland, Wales and North		South and Midlands	
	Middle class	Working class	Middle class	Working class
Conservative	70	30	75	37
Labour	30	70	25	63

Source: Butler and Stokes (1974, p. 129).
Note: The table is restricted to Conservative and Labour supporters only.

for the Liberals, which was markedly higher than average in the South West of England and in rural parts of Scotland and Wales. This continued the reputation of the Liberals as the party of the 'Celtic fringe'. Secondly, in the late 1960s there was an upsurge of political nationalism in Scotland and Wales, with the nationalist parties (SNP and Plaid Cymru) significantly increasing their support. This further heightened the electoral distinctiveness of these two countries.

Explaining regional variations in voting behaviour in Britain is a complex task and I shall return to it in Chapter 6 when I discuss post-1970 election trends. For the moment, it is worth re-emphasising that distinctive regional voting has existed for 70 years and more. This suggests that an adequate explanation will not be found by pointing to the regional effects of the policies of particular governments. Clearly, there is something more deep-seated and enduring at work. It is difficult, however, to be specific about what this something might be. Analysts often have to invoke rather vague ideas like distinctive social, religious and political traditions or distinctive cultures to explain regional electoral differentiation.

Centre−periphery theory perhaps provides a less vague general explanation (see Steed 1986). Put simply, this theory argues that British society, like some other societies, is divided into a centre or core and a periphery. The centre, London and the South East in this case, dominates the periphery culturally, economically and politically. Peripheral regions are poorer, suffer more in times of economic depression, have worse housing conditions and so on. As a result they tend to favour radical, non-establishment parties. This theory certainly does not fit the British case perfectly but it does offer some clues to understanding the geographical pattern of voting in Britain.

Butler and Stokes (1974, pp. 120—7) took their analysis of regional variations in party support a stage further by looking at the influence of the particular locality where people live. They found that the social composition of the local community affected individuals' party choice. The more middle class an area was, then the more Conservative were both middle-class and working-class voters; the more working class an area the more strongly Labour were both groups of voters. Thus a voter living in a town like St Helens, which is heavily working class, would be more likely to vote Labour than a voter of the same class living in, say, Southport. Voters, then, tend to conform to the locally dominant political norm. If almost everyone whom they meet at work and in shops, pubs and clubs appears to support the same party, then there is strong pressure on an individual to support that party too. This is sometimes called a 'neighbourhood' or 'contact' or 'contagion' effect and it is a phenomenon I shall discuss further in Chapter 6.

Class, age, sex, religion and region were the five most important socio-demographic variables influencing the British voter during the era of alignment. Voting studies, of course, investigated and provided information on a host of other variables — housing tenure, trade union membership, education, the urban—rural cleavage, car ownership and so on. To a large extent, however, these can be seen as variations on the main themes provided by the five factors I have looked at in some detail. It is worth noting, however, that race or ethnic group does not appear in the list I have given. This is because non-whites constituted a tiny fraction of the electorate during this period and little attention was paid to their voting behaviour.

Explaining the 'deviants': working-class Tories

Although occupational class was the social characteristic most strongly related to party choice (or at least to the choice between Conservative and Labour) there were, of course, many people who 'crossed over' and voted for the party of the opposite class. How could such 'deviance' be explained? Although both middle-class Labour supporters and working-class Conservatives are of interest in this respect, by far the greatest attention has been paid to the latter group. This is because working-class Tories are numerically and historically a more important group. Throughout most of the twentieth century, the working class has easily outnumbered the middle class and yet for lengthy periods Britain has been ruled by the Conservatives. They could not possibly have gained office without substantial working-class support, while Labour would never have been out of office if they had had the support of the entire working class. A number of explanations of working-class Conservatism have been put forward and I shall try to summarise them briefly.

(1)   *Cross-pressures*

One line of explanation followed the pattern established in *Voting* (Berelson et al. 1954). It suggests that working-class people are also members of other social groups — someone could be a working-class, Anglican homeowner, for example. If these other groups are Conservative-inclined, membership of them will cut across and attenuate the basic class identity of the individual. As a result, he or she will experience 'cross-pressures' and may consequently vote in a class-deviant way. The kind of conclusion to which this sort of analysis leads is illustrated (with tongue a little in cheek) by Runciman who says:

> The ideal type of the working-class Conservative is a woman in her seventies, living in a country district in the Midlands, whose father was in a non-manual occupation, who stayed on at school beyond the minimum age, who thinks of herself as 'middle class', and who would like to attend regularly at an Anglican church but is prevented by age or illness from doing so (1966, pp. 175–6).

One problem with this kind of explanation is that it amounts to little more than an exercise in probability. If, for example, 60 per cent of people having some shared social characteristic (other than class) vote Conservative, then that is interpreted as a cleavage which cross-cuts being working class. Little guidance is offered as to why some people who are members of 'cross-cutting' groups should 'defect' from their class party while others do not.

(2)   *Misperception of class position*

Class, as I have suggested, is a complex phenomenon and, although an individual may be assigned to a class by a researcher on the basis of some 'objective' characteristic such as occupation, it is frequently the case that the individual's 'subjective' view of his or her own class position is not the same as the objective categorisation. We have already seen evidence of the importance of this (Table 1.4). Runciman (1966,

Ch. 9) explores the question in some detail. He finds (p. 186) that 'manual workers and their wives who describe themselves as "middle-class" and attach some orthodox meaning to this are consistently likelier to support the Conservative Party' and explains this in terms of reference-group theory. 'Self-rated' class was a better guide to party choice than objective class but this still leaves unexplained why some members of the objective working class should fail to identify with that class and why, even among the subjective working class, there was still considerable support for the Conservatives.

(3) Deference

Two important book-length studies of working-class Conservatism (Nordlinger 1967; McKenzie and Silver 1968) reject explanations in terms of social and demographic differences within the working class, and concentrate upon attitudes — in particular, attitudes of deference. McKenzie and Silver measure deference by means of six tests and suggest that 'deferentials' are more likely to prefer political leaders of socially superior origins, assess the relative merits of the parties primarily in terms of the personal qualities of their leaders, interpret policies which benefit the working class as a consequence of the élite's goodwill or indulgence, believe that the role of ordinary voters is to confirm the right of the traditional élite to govern, uncritically accept the monarchy and the House of Lords and evaluate the Conservative party as distinctly a 'national' party. Working-class people who have these sorts of attitudes are predisposed to vote Conservative.

The concept of deference is difficult to operationalise in survey research and McKenzie and Silver's tests have been subject to criticism (see Kavanagh 1971). In any case, both McKenzie and Silver and Nordlinger find that many working-class Conservatives do not share these attitudes and, in addition, that many Labour voters are just as deferential as Conservatives. This casts doubt on the validity of the claim that deferential attitudes explain working-class Conservatism. Both studies suggest, however, that even when they were undertaken working-class deference was declining.

(4) Embourgeoisement

After Labour lost its third election in a row in 1959, many commentators believed that Labour was losing out among the working class because of growing affluence. As they became more prosperous, workers began to acquire consumer durables (like washing machines and cars), to become owner-occupiers, to go abroad for their holidays. In other words, they were becoming more like the middle class, more bourgeois, and in consequence switching politically to the Conservatives.

The 'embourgeoisement thesis' was elaborated and tested among affluent workers in Luton in 1962 by John Goldthorpe and his colleagues (Goldthorpe et al. 1968). (It is powerful testimony to the effects of inflation that a worker was deemed to be 'affluent' in 1962 if he earned £17 per week!) Goldthorpe et al. found that, contrary to the embourgeoisement thesis, affluent workers were *more* likely to be Labour supporters than were working-class people in general. They detected, however, a significant difference in the nature of the support given to Labour by affluent workers as compared with the traditional working class. Affluent workers voted Labour because they expected a Labour government to bring them direct benefits. Support was conditional and instrumental rather than 'solidaristic'. If Labour did not deliver the goods then their support would be withdrawn. Herein, perhaps, lay some of the seeds of the difficulties Labour was to encounter among working-class voters after 1970.

(5) *Political generations*

I discussed earlier the idea of political generations or cohorts. Butler and Stokes (1974) use the idea to present an 'evolutionary' view of working-class Conservatism.

In outline, the argument is that party loyalty is largely passed on from generation to generation within the family. The problem for Labour was that it was a relatively late arrival on the political scene — it was not a major national party until the 1920s. By then many families had already established patterns of support for other parties. Consequently, many people alive in the 1950s — especially older people — could not have been socialised into supporting Labour because their parents and grand-parents (more precisely, fathers and grandfathers) had established their party loyalty before Labour was on the scene. Butler and Stokes note (p. 185) that six out of seven constituencies had never had a Labour can-didate before 1919. Because of the importance of family socialisation, Conservative, or at least non-Labour, loyalties continued to be transmitted even after the emergence of Labour. There was, of course, some 'leakage' as the lines of transmission lengthened with the passage of time and Butler and Stokes suggested that on this account working-class Conservatism would decline.

This historical dimension to working-class Tory voting makes for a powerful and convincing argument — as far as the 1950s and 1960s are concerned. It is not clear that it can work for the 1970s and 1980s when the lines of transmission back to 1918 and before are very long indeed.

(6) *Asking the wrong question*

The sociologist, Frank Parkin, in a well-known article turned the whole argument about working-class Tories on its head (Parkin 1967). The problem was not, he argued, to explain why some working-class people voted Conservative but why anyone at all voted Labour! Parkin suggested that the dominant 'institutional orders' of British society — such as private property, the monarchy, the mass media, the Established Church — embody values which are in accord with Conservatism and hostile to Socialism. People exposed to these dominant or core values would be expected to vote Conservative. People can resist this psychological pressure only if they are protected, as it were, by sub-cultures formed within working-class communities, trade unions or large factories.

This is certainly an interesting way to look at the problem. Clearly, however, Parkin's analysis is less empirically based than the other explanations and it depends upon some large assumptions about the nature of the dominant value system and the connections between generalised values and electoral behaviour.

Conclusion

In Figure 2.1 I summarised the picture of the British electorate that emerged from voting studies in the 1950s and 1960s. As a result of class and partisan alignment, voters were divided into two blocs which could be relied upon to turn out in election after election to support their party. Figure 2.2 represents how the individual voter was thought of as coming to make his or her decision at elections.

This representation or model is, of course, highly simplified but it emphasises the long-term forces of class and party identification, both of which were to a large extent inherited. The significance of this was such that it made little sense to think of the voter as 'deciding' to vote for one party or another in an election. Rather the voter had a 'standing decision' or commitment to a party, and voting for it in elections was nearly automatic.

The model does not, of course, describe the voting behaviour of every single elector. As we have seen, not everyone supported their 'natural' class party and some did not identify with a party. There were always 'floating' voters who switched parties in successive elections. None the less, Figure 2.2 is the best simple representation of how the party choice of the average voter was thought to be determined in the era of alignment.

This raises a problem, however. If voting behaviour was so stable how can we account for electoral change? In the short-term, between pairs of elections, if this model were accurate we would expect little change. If we think in terms of an election transition matrix, the majority of voters would fall in the cells on the diagonal from top left to bottom right.

Table 2.7 summarises electoral change between three pairs of elections. On each occasion about two-thirds of respondents were in these cells, and most of those who were not drifted between voting and non-voting, which is also consistent with the model. Only small minorities of voters actually switched parties. None the less, it was this switching at the margins, together with the non-voting traffic, that accounted for short-term electoral change. 'Floating' of this kind appeared to be a response to rather vague short-term factors — the current images of the parties and how well governments handled the economy, for example — but, overall, floaters were less concerned and less knowledgeable about politics and less interested in the outcome of elections than were those whose voting pattern was stable. Paradoxically, it was not the politically interested and knowledgeable voters who determined which party won

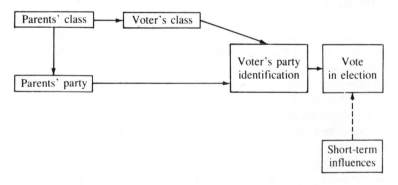

Figure 2.2   The aligned voter

Table 2.7 Constancy and change between pairs of elections, 1959–70 (%)

	1959–64	*1964–66*	*1966–70*
Voted Con. or Lab. twice	51	55	47
Voted Lib. or minor party twice	2	4	3
Did not vote twice	11	15	16
	64	74	66
Switched between Con. and Lab.	5	3	5
Switched between minor and major parties	7	4	4
Switched between voting and non-voting	24	19	25
	36	26	34

Source: Crewe (1985a, p. 110).

elections — since they were largely committed and loyal party supporters — but those whose concern with political affairs was peripheral.

According to the model, longer-term electoral change would be very slow and gradual, depending upon demographic trends (the differential fertility and mortality of the different classes, for instance) and changes in the social structure and in patterns of socialisaton. As we shall see in the next chapter, however, these expectations were not fulfilled in elections after 1970.

Notes

1. I use 'sex' rather than 'gender' because it is voting differences between the biologically defined sexes that are of interest here. Gender differences — which relate to the roles assigned to males and females — are part of the explanation for political differences between the sexes.
2. I cannot give a precise reference for this suggestion but I once heard it on a Radio 4 programme about regional accents introduced by Brian Redhead.
3. There is a story of Keir Hardie, the founder of the Labour party, haranguing a crowd of impoverished London dockers in the late nineteenth century about the merits of socialism. When he had finished he was asked, 'Yes, but what is your view on the disestablishment of the Church in Wales?'
4. Here and elsewhere the use of 'northern England' or 'the North' refers to all three northern regions — the North, the North West, and Yorkshire and Humberside.

3

The Era of Dealignment After 1970

The British electorate of the 1950s and 1960s was portrayed as aligned in two important ways. There was a partisan alignment and a class alignment. Other social characteristics also aligned with party but more weakly than class. Not surprisingly, an electorate such as that described in Chapter 2 sustained a stable two-party system. The Conservative and Labour parties dominated elections and monopolised government; electoral change was slow and small.

Even the most casual observer must have noticed, however, that in the 1970s and 1980s the party system was far from stable and electoral change was swift and extensive. As we shall see in Chapter 6, the two-party duopoly was eroded, at first by the Liberals alone and then by the Liberals in alliance with the SDP. At the same time, in Scotland and Wales the nationalist parties became established features of the political landscape. During this period electoral volatility rather than stability was conspicuous. There was even a period in the late 1970s when single-party government could not be sustained and a 'Lib-Lab' pact was required to keep the Labour government in office. Clearly something had gone wrong with the admittedly greatly simplified model of a stable, aligned electorate which I outlined in Chapter 2.

Having pictured the electorate as aligned, we can imagine that a process of *re*alignment could take place. Large sections of the electorate could stop identifying with one party and start to identify with another; some social group as a whole might switch its party allegiance. The most frequently cited example of a realignment like this is the case of black voters in the United States. Up to about 1928, when American blacks voted they usually supported the Republican party (on the perfectly reasonable grounds that President Abraham Lincoln, who freed the slaves, had been a Republican). From 1928 onwards, however, blacks began to switch to the Democratic party and today they are an over-whelmingly Democratic group.

There is no similar example of realignment in modern British political history. What largely explains the electoral turmoil of recent years, however, is a sort of half-way house between alignment and realign-ment, namely *dealignment*. This refers to a weakening of previously existing alignments. Partisan and class dealignment have been identified by numerous writers as the key processes underlying electoral behaviour during the last 20 years.

It is not, of course, that voters woke up on New Year's Day in 1970 and decided to start dealigning themselves. But 1970 does appear to be a convenient and sensible point from which to date a marked change in British electoral behaviour (see Franklin 1985, Ch. 7).

Partisan dealignment

The first trend to be considered is partisan dealignment. In Chapter 2 (Table 2.1) we saw that most electors aligned themselves with parties in the sense of identifying with them.[1] Table 3.1 shows the trends in party identification after 1970.

Table 3.1   Trends in party identification (%)

	Average 1964–70	Feb. 1974	Oct. 1974	1979	1983	1987
With party identification	90	88	88	85	86	86
With Conservative or Labour identification	81	75	74	74	67	67
'Very strong' identifiers	42	29	26	21	20	19
'Very strong' Conservative or Labour	40	27	23	19	18	16

Sources: Figures to 1979 are from Sarlvik and Crewe (1983, pp. 334–6); those for 1983 have been calculated directly from the BES 1983 data; those for 1987 are from the 1987 BES survey data, made available by Dr Heath.

The first row of the table shows that in this later period there has been a slight but perceptible decrease in the percentage of people volunteering a party identification. If, however, the question used to elicit party identification still taps long-term commitment to a party, and not just current voting intention, the decrease in such commitment is very modest.

Much more striking is the decline in the proportion whose commitment to their party is 'very strong', which is shown in the third row of the table. This has more than halved during the 1970s and 1980s. In the late 1960s more than two-fifths of the electorate thought of themselves as 'very strong' party supporters while by 1987 less than one-fifth did so. When it is remembered that stronger partisanship is associated with more stable voting, the implications of this weakening of partisan alignment are clear.

The second and fourth rows of Table 3.1 refer specifically to identification with the Labour and Conservative parties. In these cases there is again a clear decline. In the 1960s just over 80 per cent of electors identified with the two major parties but by the 1980s this had fallen to only two-thirds. This is a sharper decline than the overall drop in levels of identification, which suggests that some voters have switched their allegiance from Labour and the Conservatives. The percentage identifying 'very strongly' with either of the two parties has fallen steeply from 40 per cent of the electorate before 1970 to only 16 per cent in 1987.

On this evidence, then, people do still tend to align themselves psychologically with political parties, but they do so much less strongly than before and the predominance of the two major parties in this respect has been substantially reduced. This means that, whereas the Conservatives and Labour together used to be able to rely on solid and consistent support from about 40 per cent of the voters, their core support is now much smaller.

Explaining partisan dealignment

What explains this weakening in the intensity of support for the parties? Why are people less strongly partisan? Answers to these questions are, of necessity, speculative to some extent. They also overlap with explanations for class dealignment which, for the sake of clarity of presentation, I have tried to keep separate and shall discuss later in this chapter. If we concentrate for the moment on the weakening of partisanship, there are four main lines of explanation that can be suggested.

(1) *Increased political awareness: education*

As I noted in Chapter 2, one of the functions that identifying with a party served for the individual was to simplify the complex political world. Identification supplied 'cues' to the voter about how to evaluate policies, personalities and the actions of governments. Thus a very strong Conservative would believe, almost without thinking, that Conservative policies on taxation or health or the European Monetary System or anything else were 'good', and that Conservative leaders were 'best'; by definition the Labour party and all its works were 'bad'.

If, however, voters have become more politically aware because they are better educated, they will have less need of such a psychological device to simplify the world. And it is certainly the case, in aggregate, that over the past 25 years the electorate has received more (though some might question whether it is better) education. The school-leaving age has been raised to 16; more pupils stay on at school beyond the minimum age (and more take A-level Politics); more students now enter higher education than ever before. It is possible that as the general educational level has risen so has the level of political sophistication and, as a result, emotionally-based attachments to political parties have declined in intensity.

There is some supporting evidence at the individual level for this proposition. Crewe, Sarlvik and Alt, in their seminal study of partisan dealignment, found that the decline in partisan strength up to 1974 was most marked among those who had gone on to higher education and least marked among those who had left school at the minimum age (1977, pp. 166–7). In addition, analysis of the 1983 BES data shows that 17 per cent of respondents with some further education were 'very strong' party identifiers, compared with 21 per cent of those without further education and 27 per cent of those who left school aged 13 or 14. These data lend support to the argument that, as the electorate has slowly become more highly educated, its dependence on the 'psychological crutch' afforded by party identification has decreased.

(2) *Increased political awareness: television*

Increased political awareness and sophistication may also be a consequence of increased television coverage of politics. In the first place, it was not until the 1960s that ownership of television sets became well-nigh universal in Britain. Secondly, in its relatively short history the coverage of politics by television has changed in both extent and quality.

It may be hard to believe nowadays, but during the 1955 general election campaign television news broadcasts made no references whatsoever to the election because the broadcasting authorities feared that if they covered the election they would be in breach of the laws regulating the conduct of elections. It was only in the 1960s that campaign reports of the kind we are now familiar with began to develop. Even outside campaign periods, television coverage of politics was initially limited and circumspect in the extreme. In the first half of the 1950s there was even a rule preventing discussion on television of matters that were about to be, or had recently been, debated in the House of Commons. When leading politicians deigned to be interviewed, they determined the questions to be asked and were treated in a highly deferential manner by interviewers.

The contrast with today could hardly be clearer. Intense and detailed coverage of politics is available for those who want to watch it; MPs rush from the House to comment on debates still in progress for the benefit of the TV audience (and soon the cameras will actually be in the Commons chamber). Politicians of all parties are questioned aggressively and, indeed, if a party leader appears to have been given an 'easy ride' by an interviewer complaints are loud and long. All of this may have increased the political knowledge and sophistication of the voters and thus, indirectly, weakened party commitment.

In subtle ways the style of political television also helps to diminish the strength of partisanship. In a programme like the very popular *Question Time* we all seem to be encouraged to be Sir Robin Days, aloof from the party bickering. Partisans are projected as unreasonable ideologues and the viewer encouraged to see all sides of the story. In addition, 30 years ago very few voters would ever have seen party leaders in the flesh and they could, therefore, quite easily idealise them or else think of them as 'hate' figures. Now we see them every week on the box, and it is manifest that they are not gods or devils. Labour politicians are not, on the whole, dripping blood as they prepare to pillage the savings of the thrifty, and most Conservatives do not come over as grim-faced capitalists bent on grinding down the poor.

Even entertainment shows serve to discourage voters from thinking that their party is 'something to be loved and trusted'.[2] Impressionists poke fun at politicians and the widely viewed satirical programme *Spitting Image* holds politicians of all parties up to ridicule in a savage way.[3]

It would be very difficult, if not impossible, to measure the effects of the messages transmitted to voters by the style of political television. By their nature they are diffuse and subtle. It would be surprising, however, if the clear decline in the strength of partisan commitment over the past 20 years were unrelated to the ways in which politics and politicians have been treated by television.

(3)   *The performance of the parties*

A more direct source of weakening party identification is the apparent lack of success both major parties have had in office. Put minimally, neither has been a dazzling success. Governing a modern industrial society is a difficult and complex task, and no doubt voters are over-optimistic about what governments can achieve and too quick to blame governments when things go wrong. Nevertheless, the series of disappointments, policy failures and U-turns that have marked government performances, and the persistence of major problems facing the country, must surely have shaken any conviction voters might have had that 'their' party had all the answers.[4]

Some evidence in support of this interpretation is given in Table 3.2,

Table 3.2   Approval of government record and satisfaction with the Prime Minister and Leader of the Opposition (%)

	Approval of government record	Satisfaction with	
		Prime Minister	Opposition Leader
1951−55	49	55	—
1955−59	43	52	43
1959−64	43	51	51
1964−66	45	58	41
1966−70	31	42	33
1970−74	33	37	49
1974−79	33	46	41
1979−83	33	39	32
1983−87	34	40	38

Source: *Gallup Political Index*, 1951−87.
Note: The figures are the monthly averages of those saying that they 'approve' of the government's record to date, are 'satisfied' with the Prime Minister and think that the Leader of the Opposition is proving 'a good leader' of his or her party.

which shows that from 1966 onwards there was generally a markedly lower level of approval for the performances of governments as compared with the period 1951–64. The Labour government of 1966–70 plumbed new depths of unpopularity but even in the 1970s and 1980s approval levels remained low.

Satisfaction with the performance of political leaders has also declined. Before 1966 more than half of the electorate, on average, were satisfied with the Prime Minister; after that the figure is closer to 40 per cent. The trend in ratings for Opposition leaders is less clear, but even so they are generally lower for the period after 1966 than before.

Much wider considerations than the performances of the parties may underlie these figures. Some commentators have argued that from the late 1960s the electorate's expectations of government were unreasonably high: governments simply could not deliver what the voters expected and thus they were bound to be disappointed (see King 1975). Others suggest that there has been a decline in deference among the electorate (partly sparked off by the music of the Beatles and the Rolling Stones). People have become less trustful and willing to accept the authority of government and political leaders (Beer 1982). This relates to the argument about declining party identification, since identification itself implies a kind of deference to the authority of a political party.

(4) *Ideological disjuncture*

A final source of weakening party identification refers specifically to the Labour party. Between 1964 and 1979 there was a significant decline in support for the basic ideological principles of the Labour party, even among Labour supporters, who were themselves declining in number. Crewe (1985a, p. 138) shows that among Labour identifiers the percentages favouring each aspect of Labour's 'collectivist trinity' of public ownership, trade union power and increased spending on social welfare fell by more than 20 points between 1964 and 1979. By 1979, according to Crewe, there was an 'ideological chasm' between the Labour party and its supporters. Over an even longer period (1957–80), Martin Harrop (1982), using Gallup data, found a marked drop in the percentages of Labour voters who favoured restricting dividends and profits, cutting defence expenditure and abolishing the House of Lords.

Clearly, if there is an increasing disjuncture between the basic tenets of a party and the opinions of its supporters (let alone its potential supporters) we would expect commitment to the party on the part of its supporters to become more and more strained.

In summary, I have suggested that the progressive weakening of party identification which was shown in Table 3.1 is likely to have been a consequence of a combination of increased knowledge and sophistication about politics, the increased and changed nature of television coverage of politics, the relatively poor performances of the parties in office and the decline in support for collectivist values among Labour (and, presumably, even more so among former Labour) supporters.

Partisan dealignment has important consequences. Strong party identification was associated with stability; party choice at elections was nearly automatic. Voters who are only weakly attached to a party are likely to be more open to persuasion, more indecisive about who to vote for and more likely to switch parties. The core of support upon which each party can rely is much diminished in size. The party system, rather than being set in stone, as it were, is more unstable; its foundations are less solid and secure.

Party identification was, however, just one of the pillars of electoral politics in the 1950s and 1960s. The other was class voting and it too has been crumbling.

Class dealignment

The relationship between class (defined according to manual or non-manual status) and party choice in elections since 1964 is shown in Table 3.3.

There is a lot of information in this table which makes it somewhat difficult to interpret, but voting researchers have tried to devise summary measures of the relationship between class and vote which make comparisons over time easier. There have been two widely used measures.

The first can be calculated directly from the data in Table 3.3 and is called the 'Alford index' (since it was first used by a political scientist called Robert Alford). The index is calculated by simply subtracting Labour's percentage share of the vote among non-manual workers from its share among manual workers. Thus for 1964 the score is $(64-22)$ = 42. A little thought will show that the index can vary between 0 (equal

Table 3.3   Occupational class and party choice, 1964–87 (%)

	1964		1966		1970	
	Non-manual	Manual	Non-manual	Manual	Non-manual	Manual
Conservative	62	28	60	25	64	33
Labour	22	64	26	69	25	58
Liberal	16	8	14	6	11	9

	Feb. 1974		Oct. 1974		1979	
	Non-manual	Manual	Non-manual	Manual	Non-manual	Manual
Conservative	53	24	51	24	60	35
Labour	22	57	25	57	23	50
Liberal	25	19	24	20	17	15

	1983		1987	
	Non-manual	Manual	Non-manual	Manual
Conservative	55	35	54	35
Labour	17	42	20	45
Alliance	28	22	27	21

Sources: Heath et al. (1985, p. 30); 1987 data made available by Dr Heath.

percentages vote Labour in each class and there is, therefore, no class voting) and 100 (all manual workers vote Labour, no non-manual workers do). By convention, it is Labour voting that is used as the basis for calculating the Alford index but Conservative voting could just as easily be used.[5] The index is, then, a measure of the relative strength of a party in two classes. It is a measure of 'relative class voting'.

A second measure of class voting is the percentage of voters who support their 'natural' class party. In other words, it is the number of non-manual workers voting Conservative plus the number of manual workers voting Labour, as a percentage of all voters. This is called 'absolute class voting'. This measure cannot be derived directly from the data in Table 3.3 since to calculate it we need to know the *numbers* rather than the percentages in each cell.

Table 3.4 Measures of class voting, 1964–87

	1964	1966	1970	Feb. 1974	Oct. 1974	1979	1983	1987
Alford index (Labour)	42	43	33	35	32	27	25	25
Alford index (Conservative)	34	35	31	29	27	25	20	19
Absolute class voting	63	66	60	55	54	55	47	49

Sources: The Alford index scores are calculated from the data in Table 3.3. Absolute class voting figures are from Heath et al. (1985, p. 30) except for the 1987 figure which is calculated from 1987 BES data made available by Dr Heath.

Table 3.4 shows the Alford index scores for both parties and the level of absolute class voting in elections since 1964. All three measures indicate a decline in class voting. The Alford index scores suggest that class voting still takes place (the scores are greater than 0) but its level in the 1980s has been considerably lower than it was in the 1960s. Similarly, whereas around two-thirds of voters used to support their 'natural' class party, this is now true of less than half of the voters.

This is the basic evidence for the conclusion that over the past twenty years or so there has been a steady class dealignment among the British electorate. The same conclusion is reached by authors who have undertaken more complicated statistical analyses (see Franklin 1985, Ch. 4; Rose and McAllister 1986, Ch. 3).

Explaining class dealignment

Why has there been this weakening of the alignment between class and party choice? Explanations are, as I have indicated, very much bound up with explanations of partisan dealignment. As Crewe puts it, 'it is easier to vote against one's class once party loyalties weaken, easier to abandon one's party once class loyalties wither' (1984, p. 193). Clearly the points I made in trying to explain partisan dealignment are also relevant here. There are, however, a number of additional causes that might be pointed to. It would be naïve, of course, to expect that a phenomenon as complex as class dealignment would have one simple cause. Rather, it is a product of a series of interlocking developments.

(1) *'Son of embourgeoisement'*

In Chapter 2 I briefly discussed the testing and rejection of the 'embourgeoisement thesis' — the view that the working class was becoming bourgeois and hence Conservative — in the early 1960s. The kinds of development that led people to speculate about the possibility of embourgeoisement at that time have continued apace in the 1970s and 1980s. Despite the persistence of pockets of poverty, manual workers on the whole have become even more affluent. More and more own their own homes and consumer durables like cars, telephones and so on; many have become shareholders. At least on the surface, differences between, say, skilled manual workers and lower non-manual groups — or even traditionally solid middle-class groups like schoolteachers — are not all that obvious. If, as Goldthorpe and Lockwood found, support for the Labour party among more affluent workers is more conditional and less 'solidaristic' than it was among traditional workers, and we ally this to the voters' dim view of the performance of the parties in office, then it seems likely that the spread of affluence among the working class has created at least the potential for reduced working-class Labour voting.

(2) *Changes in the occupational and industrial structures*

The last 30 years have seen very fundamental changes in the occupational and industrial structure of Britain. Three features especially deserve to be noted. Firstly, there has been a shift from manual to non-manual work. In 1961 manual workers comprised 58 per cent of the workforce; by 1981 this had fallen to 45 per cent (Heath and McDonald 1987). For the first time, manual workers are now a minority of the workforce. To some extent the growth in non-manual employment has been associated with upward social mobility. Many people from working-class backgrounds now have professional and other non-manual occupations, and this has probably diluted the previously solid Conservative allegiance of the middle class.

Secondly, there has been a shift from employment in manufacturing to the service sector. In 1961 38 per cent of employees worked in manufacturing and 47 per cent in services. By 1981 manufacturing was down to 28 per cent and the service sector up to 62 per cent (Central Statistical Office, 1984). Put simply, there are fewer coal miners around today and more hairdressers.

Thirdly, even within manufacturing there has been an especially sharp contraction in heavy industries like coal-mining, steel, shipbuilding and textiles. These are traditionally highly unionised industries with large plants, which tended to create distinctive and homogeneous working-class communities. In contrast, the emerging 'sunrise' industries are less heavily unionised and are rarely located at the centre of established working-class communities.

Taken together, it seems likely that these sorts of change have undermined the general level of class consciousness and class solidarity which underpinned the class—party relationship.

(3) Cross-class locations

Partly as a consequence of these developments, and partly as a result of the increased proportion of women in the workforce, more and more people are in 'cross-class' locations. That is, they either individually have characteristics of more than one class or else live in mixed-class households. Thus, in the mid-1950s only about 20 per cent of manual workers were homeowners while now well over half are. On the other hand, trade union membership (traditionally a characteristic of manual workers) has increased sharply among white-collar employees. Rose (1980, p. 29) found that in 1979 only 14 per cent of the electorate conformed to a stereotype of either the middle or the working class compared with 23 per cent in 1970.

The growth of female employment (especially in non-manual jobs) has contributed to an increase in mixed-class families. By the 1970s over a third of the growing number of households in which both husband and wife had jobs were 'mixed-class' in the sense that one partner had a non-manual job while the other was a manual worker. When the effects of intergenerational mobility are added to this, the result is that more than half of all extended families — grandparents, parents and children — are mixed in their class composition. Again this reduces the potential for class solidarity in electoral behaviour.

(4) Sectoral cleavages

According to Patrick Dunleavy (1980), party choice is still basically a product of social location. What has happened, however, is that the old cleavage based on occupational class has been replaced by two new cleavages. The first relates to sector of employment — whether it is the public or the private sector — and its importance is a consequence of the sharp growth in public-sector employment in Britain (at least up to the 1980s). In 1961 24 per cent of all employees worked for the state; by 1982 the figure was 31 per cent (Dunleavy and Husbands 1985, p. 21). The second cleavage relates to sector of consumption. People who live in council houses, use public transport and depend on the NHS for medical treatment need these services to be collectively provided. They are consumers in the public sector. In contrast, people who own their own homes, use cars rather than buses or trains, and have their own medical insurance arrangements are consumers in the private sector.

The groups created by these production and consumption cleavages are in different social locations and they have conflicting interests which are translated, according to Dunleavy, into differential voting behaviour. Those in the private sectors favour the Conservatives; those in the public sectors do not.

Dunleavy's theory is not without its critics (see, especially, Franklin 1985, Ch. 2), and supporting evidence is stronger on the assumption than on the production side. None the less, the sectoral cleavage approach helps to account for the growth in non-Conservative support among white-collar employees in the public sector (such as teachers and social workers) and it provides a solid theoretical basis for the growing importance of housing tenure as a predictor of party choice.

(5) *Fragmented working-class interests*

Ivor Crewe does not subscribe entirely to the sectoral cleavage thesis, but has a somewhat similar argument. Crewe suggests that part of the explanation of class dealignment is the increased fragmentation of class (especially working-class) interests. Manual workers who are owner-occupiers or work in the private sector have different interests from those who are council tenants or public sector workers. As the tax net has widened, even moderately well-off workers have different interests (lower taxes) from the poor (higher taxes, increased welfare benefits). Workers living in the affluent and expanding South East are likely to want economic and industrial policies that are different from those favoured by people living in the North and Scotland. Workers who belong to powerful trade unions benefit from free, collective pay bargaining; those in weak unions or in none do not.

Crewe uses these sorts of difference to distinguish a 'traditional' working class (manual workers who live in Scotland/the North, are council tenants, union members and public-sector employees) and a 'new' working class (manual workers who live in the South, are owner-occupiers, private-sector employees and not union members). The 'new' working class is increasingly dominant within the working class as a whole and its support for Labour is very weak.

(6)   *Labour party success*

All the preceding explanations of the decline in class voting emphasise social change. A rather different point of view is offered by Mark Franklin (1985), whose explanation is more directly political. He argues that, paradoxically, it was the very success of the Labour government of 1945—51 which laid the basis for future problems. The Attlee government achieved Labour's 'historic mission' of eliminating grinding poverty and establishing a modern welfare state. Thereafter Labour had no sense of direction. It was no longer part of a crusade to change society but merely one among a number of parties seeking office. As such, it came to be judged like any other party on its competence and policies. While these may have continued to attract middle-class socialists, their appeal to working-class voters declined.

As I suggested above, none of these explanations by itself accounts for class dealignment. There is no single explanation. Rather, a variety of social changes and political developments have come together and interacted to produce a weakening of the class alignment.

Together, the processes of class and partisan dealignment are the most striking developments in British electoral behaviour during the last 20 years. They have produced an electorate that is very different from the electorate described by voting studies in the 1950s and 1960s. Rather than being stable and predictable so far as party choice is concerned, the voters are volatile and unpredictable. The importance of long-term forces has declined and that of short-term factors has increased.

General election results provide impressive evidence of increased voter volatility (see Chapter 6). Monthly opinion polls have also oscillated much more violently in the 1970s and 1980s than before. At the individual level, surveys have detected an increase in 'wavering' among voters (see Chapter 5). Table 3.5 compares individual volatility in two pairs of elections in the 1970s with volatility during the previous decade. It can be seen that there was a sharp fall in the proportion of voters consistently

Table 3.5 Individual constancy and change between pairs of elections (%)

	Average 1964–70	1970– 74 (Feb.)	1974– 79 (Oct.)
Voted Conservative or Labour twice	51	43	42
Voted Lib. or minor party twice	3	4	7
Did not vote twice	14	11	13
Switched between Conservative and Labour	4	5	4
Switched between major and minor party	5	8	9
Switched between voting/non-voting	23	29	25

Source: Crewe (1985a, p. 110).
Note: Figures for February to October 1974 are not given since the time between these elections was unusually short.

supporting one of the two major parties and an increase in switching between major and minor parties. Comparable figures for 1979–83 and 1983–7 cannot be given as there was no panel survey in 1983 and the panel element of the 1987 survey is not representative because of sampling variations and the loss of some respondents from the panel.[6]

'How Britain votes': a revisionist view

The argument I have put forward about the nature and importance of dealignment can be fairly described as the orthodoxy in recent British electoral studies. This view has, however, been directly challenged by Anthony Heath, Roger Jowell and John Curtice in *How Britain Votes* (1985), the British Election Study report on the 1983 general election. Their argument and analysis can be summarised in five stages.

(1) Redefinition of class

Heath et al. reject the traditional manual/non-manual dichotomy as 'wholly inadequate for studying the social bases of politics'. They also reject the market research social grading schemes (A, B, C1, etc.). Their own categorisation is based on economic interests and divides the electorate into five categories as follows:

(a) The salariat: managers, administrators, supervisors, professionals and semi-professionals.
(b) Routine non-manual: clerks, salesworkers, secretaries, 'a kind of white-collar labour force'.
(c) The petty bourgeoisie: farmers, small proprietors and own-account manual workers.
(d) Foremen and technicians: 'a kind of blue-collar élite'.
(e) The working class: 'rank and file manual employees'.

Perhaps the most striking difference between this and more common classifications is the way in which it spreads manual workers across three different groups — (c), (d) and (e). Thus, a self-employed plumber would be in group (c), a foreman plumber in group (d) and a plumber employed by a company in group (e). More traditional categorisations would classify all plumbers as skilled manual workers.

(2) *Rejection of absolute class voting*

The percentage of the electorate who support their 'natural' class party (the measure of absolute class voting) is not, claim Heath et al., a useful way of either thinking about or measuring the level of class voting. They say that this is not what commentators have in mind when they talk about the declining class basis of voting, and that as a measure it is misleading, since it is affected by the level of support which the parties obtain at particular elections. If Labour is doing badly overall, this is likely to mean that a smaller proportion of working-class people is voting Labour and in turn this will produce a decline in absolute class voting. Rather, they assert, what commentators have in mind is an increase in 'cross-class' voting — manual workers voting Conservative and non-manual workers voting Labour — that is, changes in the *relative* support for the parties in the different classes. What should be measured is relative, not absolute, class voting.

(3) *Measuring relative class voting*

Heath and his colleagues also reject the Alford index as a measure of class voting, preferring instead the 'odds ratio'. This is the odds of a person in the middle class voting Conservative rather than Labour, divided by the corresponding odds for a working-class person. Thus, using the data in Table 3.3, the odds of a non-manual worker voting Conservative rather than Labour in 1964 were 62:22 whereas for a manual worker they were 28:64. The odds ratio is, therefore, $(62/22)/(28/64) = 6.4$. The larger the odds ratio, the stronger is relative class voting.

(4) No class dealignment

Using their new class categories, Heath et al. calculate odds ratios for the salariat and the working class. The scores for elections between 1964 and 1983 are as follows:[7]

1964	9.3	Oct. 1974	6.4
1966	7.3	1979	4.9
1970	3.9	1983	6.3
Feb. 1974	6.1		

They argue that these figures do not suggest a steady decline but rather a 'trendless fluctuation' and that there is, therefore, no progressive class dealignment.

(5) Explaining Labour's decline

Proponents of the dealignment thesis use the idea of dealignment to explain the changing fortunes of the parties in recent elections and, in particular, the electoral decline of the Labour party. Since Heath and his colleagues deny that there has been a dealignment, they look elsewhere to account for Labour's lack of success. They suggest that changes in the relative sizes of the different classes have been more important than any change in the level of class voting. Between 1964 and 1983 the working class contracted while the salariat and routine non-manual classes expanded, and this alone accounts for nearly half of Labour's decline in support between these two elections.

The argument put forward by Heath, Jowell and Curtice is complicated and in places difficult to follow, although I have simplified it somewhat here. Clearly, however, their work represents a major challenge to the orthodox view about the changing relationship between class and party choice, and it is a challenge that has not gone unanswered. *How Britain Votes* has been subjected to some very vigorous criticism (see especially Crewe 1986 and Dunleavy 1987). The debate prompted by the book has become rather technical (as well as tetchy) but there are four main areas of criticism which need consideration.

Firstly, although the new class schema proposed and used in *How Britain Votes* has not in itself been greatly criticised, it is worth noting that it has the effect of 'minoritising' the working class. Between 1964 and 1983 the working class, as defined by Heath et al., declined from 47 per cent to 34 per cent of the electorate, leaving it not much larger than the salariat, which increased from 18 per cent to 27 per cent in the same period (Heath et al. 1985, p. 36). It does seem strange to use the term 'working class' to describe only one-third of the electorate, especially given that on their own figures 60 per cent of the 1983 electorate thought of themselves as working class (1987, p. 274).

There is another more technical point to be made here. In order to analyse the relationship between class and vote over time, Heath and his colleagues had to recode the occupations of all respondents to all the election surveys since 1964. They did this by computer and it seems a remarkable piece of luck that the original codings, designed with a different class scheme in mind, could all be transformed to a unique category under the new scheme, without error or even a bit of fudging at the edges. Indeed, examination of the proportion of voters coded into each of the new classes at each election suggested to Dunleavy (1987, p. 409) that 'coding consistency across the years is rather problematic'. Taken together with the sensitivity of the odds ratio (see below), this raises doubts about the trend in class voting alleged by Heath et al.

Secondly, the section in *How Britain Votes* in which the level of absolute class voting is rejected as an appropriate test of dealignment is particularly compressed and difficult to understand. If, however, by dealignment we mean something like 'a decline in the propensity of middle-class people to vote Conservative and working-class people to vote Labour', it is plain that a fall in the proportion of the electorate voting for their 'natural' class party *is* some sort of indicator of dealignment. If fewer people are voting for their class party (which Heath et al. do not deny) then the relationship between class and party is surely weakening. Moreover, Crewe (1986) effectively rebuts Heath et al.'s technical objection to the measure (that it is heavily affected by Labour's electoral fortunes) by showing that this in fact makes only a tiny difference to the scores obtained.

Thirdly, the most ferocious criticisms of Heath et al.'s analysis relate to their use of odds ratios to measure class voting. Dunleavy (1987) describes the measure as, among other things, 'quite inappropriate', 'distorting', 'peculiar', 'eccentric' and 'virtually meaningless'.

The odds ratio is highly sensitive to very small changes in the percentages used as the basis for calculation. On the basis of their sample, Heath and his colleagues estimate the ratio of Conservative to Labour voting among the salariat in 1983 as 54:14. If it had actually been 50:18, which is not greatly different, the resulting odds ratio for 1983 would be 4.5 instead of 6.3 and this might suggest a clear downward trend. The sensitivity of odds ratios is particularly important given my comments above on the problems of coding occupations and the question of sampling error mentioned in Chapter 1. Crewe (1986, p. 626) suggests that the odds ratio 'offers a spurious degree of precision and converts tiny ripples of movement — whether real or illusory — into dramatic tides of change'.

The calculation of Conservative/Labour odds also ignores support for other parties. The three situations given in Table 3.6 all produce the same odds ratio (16.0). To argue that these three situations exhibit the same level of class voting seems perverse. Heath et al. would say that they are 'controlling' for the level of third-party support but 'ignoring' it would seem a more apt description.

The odds ratios presented in *How Britain Votes*, moreover, relate only to party choice among the salariat and the working class. By 1983, however, these two classes accounted for only three-fifths of the electorate (and for less than half of all women) and, in addition, on Heath et al.'s figures it is only between these two of the five classes that there has been no steady convergence in party choice. In addition, if class dealignment were taking place we would not expect to find it most pronounced among the core components of the middle and working classes. Rather, we would expect dealignment to occur more noticeably among

Table 3.6 Class and vote: three hypothetical situations (%)

	(i)		(ii)		(iii)	
	Middle class	Working class	Middle class	Working class	Middle class	Working class
Con.	80	20	40	10	4	1
Alliance	0	0	50	50	95	95
Lab.	20	80	10	40	1	4

more peripheral groups such as routine non-manual workers or skilled manual workers.

Heath, Jowell and Curtice have defended themselves against these sorts of criticism by pointing out that their odds ratios analysis was supplemented by log-linear analysis, which they reported in footnotes and which, they claim, confirmed their conclusions. Those who are not experts in log-linear analysis have to take it on trust from those who are that it unambiguously yields the results claimed. However, the use made of the technique by Heath et al. has been subject to criticism (see Dunleavy 1987) and the fact that there is such disagreement over the application and interpretation of log-linear analysis suggests that, for the moment, appeals to it are not very convincing.

The fourth area of criticism concerns Heath et al.'s claim (p. 36) that the impact of changes in the sizes of the different classes upon the electoral performance of the parties 'has probably been far greater' than changes in the behaviour of people within the classes. No one would deny that such structural change is important, but their own calculations show that it explains less than half of Labour's decline between 1964 and 1983 and hardly anything of the rise in third-party support. Furthermore, it should have meant a rise of 5.5 points in Conservative support whereas this actually fell by 1 point. This is not exactly very impressive. In addition, Crewe (1986) demonstrates that changes in voting patterns within classes between 1964 and 1983 account for changes in the levels of support for the parties more accurately than do changes in the class structure.

Taken together, this is a powerful set of criticisms and I would conclude that the revisionist position on class dealignment advocated by Heath, Jowell and Curtice remains unconvincing. Their argument is subtle and stimulating, but the orthodox view — that class dealignment has occurred — emerges relatively unscathed.

Other social characteristics

If the influence of occupational class upon party choice has declined, what of the other social factors discussed in Chapter 2? In three cases — age, sex and religion — the relationship with party choice also seems to have weakened.

The party choice of first-time voters, the youngest age group, in each of the last three elections is shown in Table 3.7. In each case a plurality

Table 3.7 Party choice of first-time voters, 1979–87 (%)

	1979	1983	1987
Conservative	43	41	45
Labour	41	29	34
Liberal/Alliance	17	30	21

Source: Crewe (1985b; 1987).

of young people's votes has gone to the Conservatives. The stereotype of radicalism in youth no longer applies (unless to be Conservative is to be radical these days). Perhaps young people no longer have 'heart'.

Similarly, the 'gender gap' has all but disappeared (see Table 3.8). The Conservative advantage among women, a regular feature of voting in the 1950s and 1960s, is no longer apparent.

I suggested in Chapter 2 that when Butler and Stokes examined British voting behaviour, the effect of religion upon party choice was already on the wane. Since then, religious adherence and practice have declined further in Britain. It is now rarely considered in major works on electoral behaviour. There is, for example, no entry for religion in the index of *How Britain Votes*. Rose and McAllister (1986, p. 73) found that in 1983 there remained a tendency for Anglicans to be more favourably disposed to the Conservatives than members of other denomintions and people of no religion. When other social factors are taken into account, however, the influence of religious denomination almost disappears.

The fourth social influence discussed in Chapter 2 — region and locality — has increased in importance since the 1960s. The clearest evidence of this is in election results (see Chapter 6) but evidence at individual level is given in Table 3.9. This shows the differences between the support a party would be expected to receive in each region, given regional

Table 3.8 Party choice by sex, 1979–87 (%)

	1979		1983		1987	
	Men	Women	Men	Women	Men	Women
Conservative	47	47	46	43	44	44
Labour	39	39	29	29	33	31
Liberal/Alliance	13	15	24	28	22	25

Source: Crewe (1985b; 1987).

Table 3.9   Regional differences between actual and expected share of vote, 1983

	Conservative	Labour	Alliance
Scotland	−14	+6	0
Wales	−14	+14	−3
North	−5	+6	0
Midlands	+6	−2	−3
South	+6	−2	+2

Source: Calculated from Tables 6.1 and 6.2 in Heath et al. (1985, p. 75).

variations in class and housing tenure, and the actual vote reported by Heath et al.'s respondents in the 1983 election survey.

Clearly, people in Scotland, Wales and the North are notably more inclined to Labour voting and less inclined to support the Conservatives than are people who live elsewhere, even when class and housing tenure are taken into account. These regional variations are considered further in Chapter 6.

Housing tenure itself is a variable that has become more important. In the 1950s tenure was generally considered to be an aspect of class but it now appears to have a strong independent effect upon party choice. According to Rose and McAllister (1986, p. 93), tenure has been the best single social predictor of party since the election of October 1974. Heath et al. (1985, p. 45) also comment (in a rather odd phrase) that the importance of housing 'would seem to be almost greater than that of class'.

Table 3.10 shows the clear effect of housing tenure within the class categories used by Heath and his colleagues. Almost all households in Britain are either owner-occupiers (or are buying their house) or council

Table 3.10   Conservative lead over Labour by class and housing tenure, 1983

Salariat		Intermediate classes		Working class	
Owner-occupiers	Council tenants	Owner-occupiers	Council tenants	Owner-occupiers	Council tenants
+44	−3	+45	−25	+2	−42

Source: Heath et al. (1985, p. 46).
Note: Each figure is % Conservative minus % Labour in the group concerned.

tenants. Fewer than 10 per cent have other forms of tenure. The sharp differences between the two groups have been explained in two ways. Firstly, they have different or even conflicting interests. Owner-occupiers benefit from tax relief on mortgage repayments and have an interest in low mortgage rates and low domestic rates (in the pre-poll-tax days). Subsidising public housing or even simply building council housing can be seen as a 'cost' to them. Council tenants, on the other hand, do not benefit from mortgage tax relief and have an interest in keeping council rents rather than rates low.

The second explanation concentrates on socialisation processes and the neighbourhood effect mentioned in Chapter 2. People with the same housing tenure usually live in close physical promixity. There is a kind of residential segregation between council estates, modern private estates and areas of well-established substantial houses. This creates local communities in which residents interact constantly and this reinforces the dominant political values of the community.

A final social characteristic which has become more important electorally is race. Little attention was paid to the voting patterns of ethnic minorities in Britain in the 1950s and 1960s, largely because there were relatively few voters of Afro-Caribbean or Asian origin. Any national sample would have contained only a handful of such voters. However, as their numbers have increased (in particular the number of British-born ethnic minority voters), they have increased in political importance. This is highlighted by the fact that the ethnic minority population is concentrated in areas such as London, Leicester, Birmingham, Bradford and parts of the North West. As a consequence, many individual constituencies have a large ethnic minority vote. Anwar (1986) estimates that in 1987 there were 60 constituencies in which more than 15 per cent of the population belonged to ethnic minorities.

All available survey evidence shows that ethnic minority voters strongly prefer the Labour party (see Anwar 1986, Ch. 5). For example, a survey by the Commission for Racial Equality in 1983 found that 43 per cent of their white respondents voted Labour[8] compared with 86 per cent of Afro-Caribbeans and 80 per cent of Asians. This high level of Labour support is partly explicable in class terms. Voters of West Indian origin in particular are heavily working class. But Labour also attracts support from the ethnic minorities — especially Asians — because it is seen as more liberal in matters relating to race and immigration.

It remains the case, however, that ethnic minority voters constitute a small minority (about 5 per cent) of the total electorate. As a result, representative samples of the whole electorate contain too few of them for separate analysis. In addition, despite the impressively high levels of ethnic minority support for Labour, race remains a weak predictor of party choice because, of course, it does not discriminate among the large white majority.

Conclusion

In the 1970s and 1980s the British electorate, on the whole, moved from aligned to dealigned voting. This is not to say that voters became entirely free-floating, as it were. Rather, there was a marked diminution in the intensity of psychological commitment to the two parties which had previously dominated elections, and in the strength of the relationship between an individual's position in the social structure and his or her party choice. Although new cleavages have emerged, like race, and others continue to be important, like region, voting is no longer so firmly anchored in the social structure. The success rate one would achieve in predicting party choice from knowledge of a person's class, age, sex or religion has steadily fallen. There still remains *some* alignment but its most striking feature is its weakness, not its strength.

This immediately raises a question. If voters no longer receive powerful cues about which party to support from a long-standing party identification or from their social location, how do they now decide? Answers to this question are considered in the next chapter.

Notes

1. There is some confusion in the literature over the precise meaning to be attached to the term 'partisan alignment', and the distinction to be made between this and 'class alignment'. There is general agreement, however, that weakening party identification is a sign of partisan dealignment. It seems logical, therefore, to use 'partisan alignment' to refer to a situation in which voters align themselves psychologically with parties by identifying with them. Such a situation could, of course, exist without an accompanying class alignment.
2. This phrase was used of political parties a long time ago by Graham Wallas (1910).
3. The popularity of David Steel, the leader of the Liberal party, fell sharply between 1983 and 1987, and many people attributed this in part to the way he was portrayed in *Spitting Image* — as fawning upon and being treated with derision by the leader of the SDP, David Owen.

4. I once interviewed a voter in the late 1960s, when the current Labour government was highly unpopular. He was a Labour identifier but when asked about his strength of identification his reply was 'Getting weaker every day!'

5. In this case, of course, we would subtract the % Conservative among manual workers from the % Conservative among non-manuals.

6. For interest, however, the following rates of constancy and change were reported in the 1983 and 1987 cross-section samples. The figures are based on respondents' recall of what they did four years before and this tends to exaggerate the extent of constancy.

	1979–83 (%)	1983–87 (%)
Voted Con. or Lab. twice	52	54
Voted Lib./Alliance or minor party twice	7	10
Did not vote twice	5	5
Switched between Con. and Lab.	4	3
Switched between major and minor party	14	13
Switched between voting and non-voting	18	15

7. The figure given for October 1974 is not the same as that given in *How Britain Votes* but is based on corrected figures reported later by Heath et al. (1987).

8. The survey was conducted in mainly Labour-held constituencies.

4

The Rise of Issue Voting

If a political commentator or politician of the 1920s or 1930s were able to read the previous two chapters he or she would be utterly amazed at the relative lack of attention paid to party policies or to topical events and political issues. Before survey studies of voting behaviour began, elections and voting were conceived of in terms of choices between competing policy proposals. The voter was pictured as weighing up the policies of the different parties, and on that basis deciding which party to vote for. The party which won an election was thought to have a 'mandate' from the electorate for all of its policy proposals detailed in its election manifesto. In the nineteenth century John Stuart Mill said this about the voter:

> His vote is not a thing in which he has an option ... he is bound to give it according to his best and his most conscientious opinion of the public good ... the voter is under an absolute moral obligation to consider the interest of the public, not his private advantage, and give his vote to the best of his judgement exactly as he would be bound to do if he were the sole voter and the election depended upon him alone (1963, pp. 302–4).

This idealised view of the voter informed much comment upon elections until well into the twentieth century.

In the first two chapters, in contrast, I have considered voting behaviour as almost entirely a function of social and even psychological processes, hardly mentioning party policies or 'the interest of the public'. It would, of course, be going too far to claim that not a single voter decided how to vote after carefully evaluating the parties' policies or that policy considerations played no part at all in the decision processes of most voters.

71

The Michigan model explicitly contains 'issue orientation' as a short-term factor affecting party choice and most studies of British voters found that they did have generalised images of the parties that were not without policy content. Thus the Labour party was widely perceived as the party which was 'for the working class' or in favour of nationalisation and higher welfare spending. None the less, when researchers tried to be more precise about the effects of electors' political opinions upon their voting choices, their results did not suggest that there was a very strong connection between the two.

Conditions for issue voting

Following Butler and Stokes (1974), there are four conditions that must be met if an issue is to affect voting and a voter is to qualify as an 'issue voter':

(1)   The voter must be aware of the issue concerned. Clearly if someone failed to notice that the Falklands War took place in 1982 then that issue could not have affected his or her vote in a subsequent election.

(2)   The voter must have some attitude to or opinion about the issue. I might be well aware that people have strong views about whether or not Britain should apply economic sanctions to South Africa but be completely indifferent myself or else unable to make up my mind. In these cases the issue could not affect my vote.

(3)   The voter must perceive different parties as having different policies on the issue. Again, if this is not the case, there is no logical way in which the voter's opinion on the issue can be related to the choice of a party in an election. In the 1960s, for example, many voters had strong opinions on the question of immigration but believed that there was no difference between the parties on the issue. As a result, the issue did not, on the whole, affect voting behaviour (see Butler and Stokes 1974, pp. 303–8).

(4)   Finally, and obviously, the voter must vote for the party whose position on the issue is, or is perceived to be, closest to his or her own position.

Two further points about the role of issue opinions in elections should be noted. Firstly, the four conditions need to apply for an individual to be an issue voter, but for an issue to affect the outcome of an election many voters have to fulfil the conditions and, in addition, opinion on the issue must be skewed. If roughly the same number of people are for and against some policy, and vote on that basis, the policy will make little difference to the net strength of the parties. If, however, one side of the issue has much wider support than the other, and the other conditions are met, then the overall election result will be altered by the issue.

Secondly, the kinds of issue I have had in mind here are 'position' issues. People take positions for and against sanctions against South Africa, capital punishment, unilateral nuclear disarmament or whatever (although, of course, on many issues there are more than two possible positions). As Butler and Stokes (1974, p. 292) point out, however, there are many issues on which there is broad agreement among the electorate about the goals government should pursue. What is at issue is the competence or performance of the parties in seeking to achieve these goals. Not many people, for example, are in favour of increased crime or against peace and prosperity, but there would be disagreement about which party would be most likely to be successful in combatting the former and promoting the latter. Butler and Stokes call these sorts of issue 'valence' issues.

Issue voting in the era of alignment

When aligned voting was the norm in Britain, relatively few voters qualified as issue voters. Firstly, on the question of awareness of issues, studies consistently found that large numbers of electors managed to get through life with only the haziest notion about the nature of the issues exercising the interest of MPs, political correspondents and lobby correspondents and little understanding of the language in which political debate was conducted. Butler and Stokes comment that 'the simplest evidence about the extent of popular attention to the affairs of government must challenge any image of the elector as an informed spectator. Understanding of policy issues falls away very sharply indeed as we move outwards from those at the heart of political decision-making to the public at large' (p. 277). In 1964, 40 per cent of respondents to the BES survey were unable to name two important questions facing the country (quoted in Franklin 1985, p. 128). Politics and political issues were simply peripheral to most people's concerns.

Butler and Stokes also cast doubt on the extent to which, even when they were aware of issues and were prepared to nominate the position they held, electors actually had genuine attitudes towards issues and policies. They illustrate this by reference to the question of nationalisation. This is an issue which had been at the centre of political controversy in Britain for a long time and on which there were clearly perceived differences between the parties. Yet over four separate interviews, less than half (43 per cent) of Butler and Stokes' respondents were consistent in either supporting or opposing further nationalisation. In addition, when Butler and Stokes investigated the extent to which voters' opinions on eight different issues were interrelated, they found that opinions did not 'hang together' in the way that a sophisticated observer would expect. Thus, opinions on whether trade unions had too much power were not systematically related to opinions about whether big business was too powerful. Even when they restricted their analysis to respondents who had constant opinions over time on each issue — only 30 per cent of the sample — Butler and Stokes concluded that 'the main impression left . . . is of the weakness of the links between attitudes . . . even when we go to such lengths to confine our attention to the minority of people who have well-formed and enduring views, the association of attitudes is relatively feeble' (p. 320).

Perception of differences between the parties on issues (the third condition for issue voting) varied very much depending upon the nature of the issue. On 'big' or broad issues, like welfare spending or nationalisation, voters were mostly able to see a difference between the Conservatives and Labour, but on a whole series of more precise, technical or esoteric policy questions (and on immigration as noted earlier) this was not the case. In addition, voters were notably unable to assign policy stances to the Liberals.

Finally, even voters who successfully passed the first three issue-voting tests frequently fell at the last fence. Despite having an opinion which they knew was contrary to a party's policy, some would nevertheless go ahead and vote for that party. This was particularly true of Labour supporters, a majority of whom were regularly found to oppose the party's policy of nationalisation. A survey of Bristol voters in 1955 (Milne and MacKenzie 1958) found that 39 per cent of Labour voters were pro-Conservative in their policy preferences with a further 27 per cent being neutral.

In sum, then, voting in the era of alignment can fairly be described as virtually 'issueless'. Voters were as likely to change their policy preferences to fit their party as they were to change their party to fit their policy position. There was, of course, *some* issue content in voting decisions and some electors were, no doubt, fully-fledged issue voters. But using the criteria suggested by Butler and Stokes, issue voting was the exception rather than the rule. To that extent, voting studies were justified in emphasising the social and psychological bases of voting behaviour.

We have seen, however, that the social underpinnings of party choice have crumbled and partisan attachment has weakened. In these circumstances, issue voting has grown in importance. Some of the factors explaining partisan dealignment — such as increased political awareness and exposure to politics on television — have also increased the propensity of electors to vote on the basis of their policy preferences.

This is not as straightforward as it might appear, however. As more and more attention has been paid to the role of issues in elections, doubts and disagreements have emerged about the meaning and measurement of issue voting.

Measuring issue voting

There is no consensus about what issue voting should be called. The terms used include 'policy voting', 'consumer voting', 'instrumental voting' and 'ideological voting'. Two variants on the basic model are 'investment voting' and 'retrospective voting'. All of these are inspired, in part at least, by rational choice theory (see Downs 1957), and involve the voter making a calculated decision about which party to support (or even about whether to vote at all) on the basis of his or her policy preferences and assessments of the parties' positions or performance.

The increased concern with issue voting on the part of researchers has focused attention upon two important methodological difficulties. The first relates to the problem of causation. How do we know whether a voter selects a party on the basis of his or her policy preferences or general ideological stances (as the model requires), or whether the voter first picks a party and then adjusts his or her position to fit the party's policies? This problem gets even more complex if we allow other variables to come into the reckoning. For example, Figure 4.1 shows three possible relationships between social location, policy preferences and party choice.

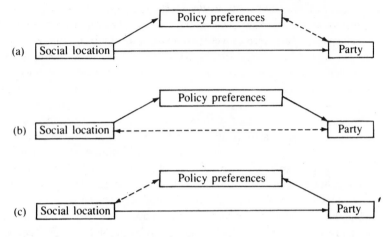

Note: Unbroken lines indicate causal paths.

Figure 4.1 Social location, preferences and party choice: three possible relationships

In example (a) social location determines party choice and, independently, a person's policy preferences. The effect is that there is a relationship between policy preferences and party but it is accidental. Preferences do not 'cause' party choice. In example (b) a particular social location gives rise to particular policy preferences which in turn determine party choice. Here it is the social location/party relationship which is spurious. Finally (example (c)) it is possible that social location determines vote and that voters then adjust their policy preferences in the light of this. (The voter's reasoning might be: 'I've decided to vote Conservative, the Conservatives favour privatisation, so I favour privatisation.')

There is no simple way of resolving the problem of causal direction empirically. We can demonstrate the extent to which voters fulfil the conditions for issue voting, but ultimately it cannot be proved that issue preferences cause or determine party choice.

The second methodological problem is sometimes referred to as the problem of 'decision rules' or 'trade-offs'. A voter might be pro-Conservative on some issues (say, privatisation), pro-Labour on others (say, welfare spending) and pro-Democrat on others (reforming the electoral system perhaps). The difficulty is that we do not know how the issue voter decides which issues are the ones that will determine his or her vote. How does a voter 'trade off' a preference for changing the electoral system against a preference for privatising nationalised industries?

The problem can be illustrated from a survey of school sixth-formers carried out by myself and a colleague. We found that 3,354 of our respondents favoured more spending on the health service to be financed by increased taxes. This is broadly a Labour position. But 45 per cent of these also supported the Conservative position on defence (opposition to unilateral nuclear disarmament), and 47 per cent favoured electoral reform (an SLD policy). Twenty per cent of those who preferred the Labour position on health preferred the Conservatives on defence *and* the SLD on electoral reform. Clearly, many people's policy preferences do not all point in the same direction.

The commonest way out of this problem is simply to tot up the balance of voters' preferences over a number of issues. But this is not entirely satisfactory, since it involves imposing a decision rule under which all issues are weighted equally when in reality a voter's feeling on one issue may outweigh his or her preferences on all others.

Evidence of increased issue voting

In a series of reports on general elections Ivor Crewe (1981a, 1985b, 1987b) has developed a distinctive and simple way of analysing issue voting. This involves, firstly, the *salience* of different issues, that is, the extent to which they are in people's minds. This is indicated by the percentage of voters mentioning an issue as one they thought important when they were deciding how to vote. Secondly, there is the *party preferred* on the issue — the party which is thought to have the best policy. The third factor is the *credibility* of party proposals — the extent to which voters believe that parties will or will not be able to achieve their policy goals.

Table 4.1 shows the figures Crewe has presented on issue salience and party preference on issues for the last four elections. One fascinating feature of the table is the way in which it charts the rise and fall of various issues. Unemployment is the only one to appear in all four elections. The Common Market, on the other hand, has now disappeared as an issue. Defence policy became salient only in the 1983 election. Crewe's contention is that the outcomes of these elections can largely be explained by a combination of changes in the salience of issues and changes in the electorate's judgements about the party which has the best policies

Table 4.1 Issues in elections, 1974–87

	Oct. 1974		1979	
	Salience	Preferred party lead	Salience	Preferred party lead
Prices	82	Lab. +11	42	Lab. +13
Unemployment	12	Lab. +19	27	Lab. +15
Trade unions/ strikes	15	Lab. +33	20	Con. +15
Common Market	11	Con. +3	—	—
Taxes	—	—	21	Con. +61
Law and order	—	—	11	Con. +27

	1983		1987	
	Salience	Preferred party lead	Salience	Preferred party lead
Prices	20	Con. +40	—	—
Unemployment	72	Lab. +16	49	Lab. +34
Defence	38	Con. +54	35	Con. +63
NHS	11	Lab. +46	33	Lab. +49
Education	—	—	19	Lab. +15

Sources: Gallup data reported in Crewe (1981a, 1985b, 1987b).
Note: The table reports issues mentioned by more than 10% of voters at any of the four elections. The preferred party's lead is % saying the party most preferred on the issue overall had the best policy minus % saying the same of the next most preferred party.

on the issues, together with voters' assessments of the credibility of party policies.

In October 1974 Labour was clearly ahead on three of the four major issues and won the election. In 1979 the Conservatives pushed taxation and law and order on to the election agenda and recorded huge leads on these issues. In addition, the electorate's firm preference for Labour on trade union matters in 1974 changed to a preference for the Conservatives in 1979 and, although Labour still led on prices, this issue had become much less salient. This combination was enough to win the election for the Conservatives. Crewe concludes that in 1979 'it was issues that won the election for the Conservatives ... the Conservatives' success came from saying the right things about the right issues' (1981a, pp. 282–3).

In the 1983 election, unemployment was the most salient issue and

Labour was the preferred party on the problem. But Crewe found that Labour's credibility was weak — the voters did not think that Labour could achieve what they actually promised on unemployment. Their leads on this issue and on the NHS were outweighed by large Conservative leads on defence policy and prices.

This line of analysis runs into difficulties, however, when it is applied to the 1987 election. Labour had a clear lead on three of the four most salient issues — unemployment, NHS and education. Despite the enormous Conservative lead on defence, if electors had voted on the basis of their preferences on these issues Labour would have won the election — but, of course, they lost decisively.

In attempting to resolve this paradox Crewe shifts his ground somewhat as compared with his previous analyses. He argues that in 1987 voters were mainly concerned with their own private prosperity and the Conservatives were seen as the party most likely to create or maintain prosperity. 'Here', says Crewe, 'quite simply and obviously, lies the key to Conservative victory.'

Issue voting is still implicit in this argument but the issue concerned, prosperity, is a valence issue. Prosperity is not a 'problem' but a goal and the voters opted for the party they judged most likely to attain it. I mentioned 'investment voting' earlier and this is an example of it. The voters, according to Crewe, invested in future prosperity after calculating which party was likely to yield the best return. There is, too, some 'retrospective' element since expectations about the future are to some extent based on experience of the past performances of the parties.

Crewe's method of analysing issue voting in these reports has been severely criticised. The survey question used to find out which party a respondent prefers on an issue is some variant of 'which party do you think would be best at dealing with [the issue concerned]?' This is a heavily loaded question, in that if people are going to vote for a particular party they are likely to say that it is best on practically anything, without necessarily even knowing what the party's policies are. In Crewe's defence, it could be said that the fact that different parties are preferred on different issues casts doubt on this. In any event, Crewe's election reports are not intended to be rigorous tests of the issue-voting model but explanations of the outcomes of particular elections.

Fortunately Crewe, together with Bo Sarlvik, has provided a much more exhaustive analysis of issue voting in the 1970s (Sarlvik and Crewe 1983). The complexity and extensiveness of their analysis make it difficult to summarise, but for our purposes a number of points stand out. The relevant data are presented in Tables 4.2 and 4.3.

Table 4.2 Issue opinions and party choice in the 1979 General Election

	% who have position	% who locate Con. and Lab. differently	Correlation: opinion/ party (a)	Correlation: opinion/ party (b)	Correlation: opinion/ party (c)
Tax cuts v. govt services	87	80	0.25	0.33	0.44
How to tackle unemployment	85	82	0.35	0.42	0.46
Incomes policy	87	73	0.00	0.32	0.42
Laws to regulate trade unions	87	83	0.41	0.47	0.62
EEC economic policies	80	66	0.11	0.24	0.47
Improving race relations	87	70	0.07	0.19	0.36
Social services	98	83	0.28	0.39	0.51
Nationalisation	94	88	0.45	0.48	0.60

Source: Sarlvik and Crewe (1983, pp. 190–1, 208–9, 213, 217, 223).
Notes: The correlations shown between issue opinion and party choice in column (b) refer to voting for the 'closest' party as explained in the text. Those given in column (c) are for voters who considered the issue 'extremely important'. The coefficients are Tau-b coefficients which have essentially the same meaning as the correlation coefficient discussed in Chapter 1.

Table 4.3 Valence issues and party choice in the 1979 General Election

	Average % assessing Con. and Lab.	Correlation: assessment/ party (a)	Correlation: assessment/ party (b)
Strikes	96	0.52	0.53
Rising prices	97	0.52	0.60
Unemployment	95	0.51	0.56
Law and order	96	0.39	0.44

Source: Sarlvik and Crewe (1983, pp. 154–6, 161, 223).
Notes: The correlations given in column (b) are for respondents who considered the problem 'extremely important'. As in Table 4.2, the coefficients are Tau-b coefficients.

Sarlvik and Crewe analysed opinions on six issues (the first six shown in Table 4.2) by asking respondents to choose between two policy alternatives in each case. In the cases of the two other issues (social services and nationalisation) four alternatives were offered. The first column in the table relates to the first two conditions for issue voting — there must be an awareness of the issue and the voter must have some position on it. Clearly, very large majorities nominated their policy preferences in each case, the lowest being 80 per cent on how Britain should respond to EEC economic policies. The third step in the issue-voting model — perceiving the parties as having different positions — is tested in the second column. On three issues (incomes policy, reaction to EEC policies and improving race relations) the percentage of respondents able to differentiate the Conservative and Labour parties' positions is somewhat smaller than in the other cases. This is not surprising since the parties' positions themselves were not entirely clear. Overall, substantial majorities pass the third condition for issue voting.

The third column of the table concerns the relationships between people's opinions on policy and their vote — whether it was Conservative, Liberal or Labour. Correlation coefficients are used to measure this (see Chapter 1) and it is clear that although opinions on some issues are poor predictors of party choice (incomes policy, the EEC and race relations) the others show significant positive relationships. That is, policy opinions are clearly related to party choice.

This is not, however, strictly what is meant by issue voting. What we need to know is the extent to which people vote for the party which they *believe is closest* to their view on the issue concerned. The correlations between opinion and voting for the 'closest' party in this sense are shown in the fourth column of the table and in every case the coefficients are larger than those in the third column.

Finally, Sarlvik and Crewe tackle the problem of 'decision rules' discussed earlier. They group respondents according to their rating of each issue as 'extremely important', 'fairly important' or 'not very important', and find that for each issue the correlations between issue position and party choice are regularly strongest among respondents who consider the issue extremely important and weakest among those who consider it not very important. The figures for those who rate each issue as 'extremely important' are given in the fifth column of Table 4.2, and they are sharply higher than the corresponding figures for all respondents shown in the third column.

Unfortunately, Sarlvik and Crewe do not provide figures for 'closest party' voting taking account of the importance attached to the issue, but the presumption must be that these correlations would be stronger still. They do, however, consider the combined impact of issue opinions by means of a multiple-regression analysis. Taking all eight issues together produces a multiple correlation coefficient of 0.68 between issue opinion and party choice.

Another part of Sarlvik and Crewe's analysis concerns four valence issues — strikes, unemployment, prices, and law and order. These are valence issues since few people would actually favour more strikes, heavier unemployment, higher prices or public disorder, and what issue voters do in these cases is assess the relative competence of the parties in handling these problems. As Table 4.3 shows, almost all respondents in 1979 were willing to offer assessments of the ability of the Conservative and Labour parties to handle the problems. The correlations between these assessments and party choice are consistently strong (although stronger in the case of economy-related issues than for law and order) and they increase in strength when only those who thought an area 'extremely important' are considered. Combining assessments on prices, strikes and unemployment produced a multiple r of 0.69.

Now, what do all these statistics mean? On the basis of this summary of Sarlvik and Crewe's work it is difficult to judge exactly how important issue opinions are in determining party choice, but two further points from their study put issue voting into perspective and give a clearer indication of its importance. Firstly, comparing the effect of policy opinions and assessments with the effect of social characteristics on party choice, they say that 'the voters' opinions on policies and on the parties' performances in office "explain" more than twice as much as all the social and economic characteristics taken together' (p. 113). Secondly, using a statistical technique known as *discriminant analysis*, they find that the votes of 69 per cent of their respondents can be correctly predicted on the basis of their issue opinions and assessments. If only those predicted to vote for the two major parties are considered (it is notoriously difficult to predict third-party voting), 86 per cent of respondents actually voted for the party that was predicted on the basis of their political opinions.

One drawback of Sarlvik and Crewe's analysis of issue voting is that it lacks an over-time perspective. While they do make some comparisons with the 1974 elections, and in particular compare the issue opinions of stable voters with those of 'switchers', their main focus is on the 1979 election. To substantiate the claim that issue voting has increased as

Table 4.4 Contribution of issue opinions to explaining party choice

1964	1966	1970	1974	1979	1983
25.8	26.7	39.1	36.3	40.1	39.6

Source: Franklin (1985, p. 145).
Note: The figure for 1974 is the average of the two elections of that year.

aligned voting has decreased, we really require an analysis covering a series of elections since the 1960s.

This is provided by Mark Franklin (1985). Here, it must be said, the statistical techniques involved are very complicated indeed and Franklin faced formidable problems in finding data that were exactly comparable over time. None the less, the main point made by Franklin can be easily grasped without necessarily understanding the detailed statistics involved. Using the BES series of election surveys, Franklin takes account of a variety of influences upon party choice — issue opinions, social class, party identification, parents' class and parents' party — and calculates the percentage contribution that issue opinions make to explaining party choice. The figures are shown in Table 4.4. As can be seen, the importance of issues from 1970 onwards is substantially greater than it was before.

The debate about issue voting

If 'aligned voting' was the orthodoxy of electoral analysis in the 1950s and 1960s, issue voting has been the orthodoxy of the 1970s and 1980s. All orthodoxies invite challenge, however, and proponents of the issue-voting model have themselves come in for criticism.

Heath et al. (1985) again cast themselves as revisionists. In *How Britain Votes*, they describe issue voting as a 'vogue' and in a remarkably brief chapter dismiss the argument that people vote on the basis of their policy opinions. Their conception of issue voting, which they call 'consumer voting', is, however, very narrow. They describe it as relating to 'the detailed stands which competing parties take on issues of the day' (p. 89), 'detailed appraisals of party manifestos and policies' (p. 99) and 'the small print of the manifesto' (p. 107). Few of those who argue that there has been an increase in issue voting would conceive of it in these terms.

In their discussion of 'consumer voting', Heath et al. do not take the voters' judgements about the performance or competence of parties into account, on the grounds that these judgements are inextricably bound up with party preference. If Labour voters think Labour is best at dealing with unemployment this is because they are Labour voters. The judgement is a consequence of the party choice, not a cause of it. Heath et al., therefore, concentrate on position issues and find that, if people had voted in the 1983 general election for the party which they saw as closest to them on the issue they considered most important, the election would have resulted in a dead-heat between Labour and the Conservatives. Since Labour was in fact trounced, the policy-voting model can be rejected.

Heath et al.'s test is interesting but it does not tell us anything about the prevalence of issue voting among the electorate. They do not report the proportion of voters whose vote could be correctly predicted on the basis of their opinions on policies and their perceptions of the parties' stands on them. Because they see no logic in imposing a 'decision rule' about the weight attached to different issues, they do not attempt to construct any kind of index which would summarise a person's issue preferences and then see how this relates to party choice.

Heath et al. argue that voters do not choose a party on the basis of policy preferences, but on the basis of their 'general values and their overall perceptions of what the parties stand for' (p. 107). This is itself a rather general statement and in trying to be more specific it seems to me that Heath and his colleagues get into something of a pickle. To demonstrate the existence and role of these general values they rely on answers to questions about issues and policies. The issues which they find to be most important in differentiating between Conservative and Labour supporters are nationalisation, trade union legislation, income redistribution, defence spending, private education and job creation (p. 109). Not all of these were campaign issues in 1983, say Heath et al., but rather they are bound up with the overall images of the parties and 'constitute the main ideological divisions between the parties' (p. 109). The Labour party, for example, is recognised as the party favouring nationalisation, the trade unions, equality and so on, irrespective of the particular issues of the day. So while they utilise responses to issue questions, Heath et al. see them as 'not so much tapping discrete issues as a general ideological dimension' (p. 111). The fact remains, however, that nationalisation, defence spending and the rest *are* issues. They are matters of public policy about which the parties disagree and Heath and his colleagues do not present any evidence that people's opinions on these issues intercorrelate in a way that would be expected if they did indeed subscribe to a set of general values.

A somewhat similar account to that given by Heath *et al.* is put forward by Rose and McAllister (1986). They too reject the view that issues, which they define as 'topical issues of the moment, which are transitory by definition' (p. 117), are an important influence on voting behaviour. They say (p. 147) that 'how a person votes is a poor guide to what a person thinks about most issues today' (and, presumably, vice versa). What are important, according to Rose and McAllister, are the 'political principles' which voters hold. Principles are 'underlying judgements and preferences about the activities of government [which] are general enough to be durable ... [and] ... concern persisting problems of public policy' (p. 117).

Rose and McAllister use a technique called *factor analysis* to explore patterns in voters' responses to questions on eleven enduring issues in British politics (nationalisation, spending on the health service, etc.) at three separate elections. They identify four principles that appear to underlie opinions and they call these socialism, welfare, traditional morality and racialism. These are distinct principles in the sense that answers to questions dealing with welfare, for example, intercorrelate highly but are not related to opinions in the other three areas.

Only one of Rose and McAllister's principles — socialism — importantly affects party choice. The effect is to penalise Labour since most voters are anti-socialist. The others have only a slight effect on party choice — indeed there is 'intra-party consensus' on them among voters (pp. 124–5).

The method used by Rose and McAllister to analyse the effects of opinions has been sharply criticised by Johnston and Pattie (1988). Using the same survey data for the 1983 election as Rose and McAllister, Johnston and Pattie use discriminant analysis to show that on the basis of political opinions the votes of 81 per cent of Conservatives, 67 per cent of Labour voters and 55 per cent of Alliance voters can be correctly predicted. They say that 'this hardly sustains a conclusion that what people think is a poor predictor of how they vote: quite the opposite' (p. 30).

Despite their apparent rejection of the issue-voting model, however, Rose and McAllister do agree that voters' opinions have increased in importance in explaining party choice, even after allowing for the effects of social characteristics and parental influence. Their analysis shows that, taken together, the voters' political principles and judgements about the current performances of the parties are now easily the most important determinants of party choice. Rose and McAllister conclude:

> Voters are increasingly open to political influence. In 1974, 40 per cent
> of the variance [in vote] was explained by political principles and the cur-
> rent performance of parties, 10 per cent more than by social structure.
> By 1983, 50 per cent of the variance was explained by political principles
> and the current performance of parties, 23 per cent more than that explained
> by social structure (p. 133).

Heath et al. and Rose and McAllister are at pains to emphasise their rejection of issue or consumer voting. In fact, however, the model of issue or consumer voting that they reject is something of a straw man. They insist on defining issue voting narrowly, restricting 'issues' to 'tran- sitory' matters to be found in the 'small print' of party manifestos or talked about by parties during election campaigns. It seems sensible, however, to think of issues as lying on a continuum as shown in Figure 4.2.

At one extreme some issues are highly specific and transitory. Examples might be the question of whether the Inner London Education Authority should be abolished or drinking beer in public banned. At the other extreme there are general questions about how society should be organised and these persist over time. Is equality a desirable goal? Should the state or the private citizen be responsible for the provision of health care? Both sorts of question are concerned with issues. Both concern public policy and are matters over which people and political parties disagree. Other issues would fit somewhere on the continuum, depend- ing on their level of generality and durability.

Although they might deny it, Heath et al. and Rose and McAllister can be said to subscribe to a kind of issue voting. The difference be- tween them and other writers is that their 'general values' or 'political principles' are to be found towards the right-hand end of the continuum while others are more concerned with issues located from the centre to the left-hand end.

Specific   General
transitory   durable

Figure 4.2   A continuum of issues

Conclusion

The decline of the alignment between social-structural characteristics and party choice, as well as the decline of strong party identification, has not left a vacuum in which voters make almost random choices among competing parties. Rather, voting is now structured by opinions. As aligned voting has declined, the 'gap' has been at least partly filled by opinion voting. The average British voter of the 1980s (if there is such a person) is strikingly different from the average voter of the 1950s. Today, the voter is much more knowledgeable about political issues, more likely to have opinions about them, more aware of the parties' positions on them and more likely to vote (or not vote) for a party on policy or performance grounds.

5

Party Leaders, Election Campaigns and the Media

When the votes cast in the 1945 general election were being counted, the leader of the Labour party, Clement Attlee, attended the count in his constituency in the East End of London. After his result was declared (he won easily), Attlee got into his car and drove himself to Labour party headquarters. Later the same day it became clear that Labour had won the election and the incumbent Prime Minister, Winston Churchill, went to Buckingham Palace to resign. Five minutes later Attlee drove himself to the Palace, kissed hands and became Prime Minister.

The idea of a major party leader driving himself around in this way would be inconceivable today. During election campaigns party leaders are whisked hither and thither by aeroplane, helicopter, battle-bus or car with an entourage of personal staff, security personnel, newspaper reporters, television crews and assorted other hangers-on. This is because general election campaigns are now focused more on the party leaders. Campaign managers have to ensure that the party leaders project a good image. Their itineraries are planned in detail, the meetings they address carefully controlled, they are coached on how to perform well on television, advised on how to dress, how to have their hair cut and so on. Mrs Thatcher has even deliberately lowered the pitch of her voice in order to create a more favourable impression upon the voters.

Developments of this kind have led to claims that general elections are becoming more presidential in character. They are portrayed as contests between candidates for Prime Minister rather than between political parties competing for control of government. Of course, electoral politics have always been personalised to some extent — elections in the second half of the nineteenth century could be portrayed as contests between Gladstone and Disraeli, for example. What is relatively new is the intensive exposure of party leaders on television. Given this, however, it is necessary to consider the impact of party leaders on electoral behaviour.

The impact of the leaders

In the previous three chapters I have agued that there has been a major change in electoral behaviour in Britain — from aligned to dealigned voting. On that basis we might expect that there has also been a change in the impact of party leaders.

In the period of alignment, our expectation would be that the personalities of leaders would have had relatively little electoral effect. The original Michigan model did allow for 'candidate orientation' as a short-term influence on party choice but that model was, of course, developed with presidential rather than parliamentary elections in mind. In Britain, the long-term forces of social class and family socialisation would be presumed to have overriden the purely temporary consideration of who happened to be the leader of each party. Indeed, we would expect voters' assessments of the party leaders to have been themselves products of basic party loyalty. On the whole, each party's supporters would have approved of its leader and disapproved of the others.

With the erosion of the importance of long-term factors, however, we might expect an increase in the electoral impact of party leaders. The competence, personality and image of individual leaders might be regarded as akin to issues which could swing votes in the short term.

There are, as might be expected, problems in assessing the precise impact of party leaders. It is difficult to disentangle electors' views about the leader of a party or Prime Minister from views about the party or the government. Judgements on individual politicians will almost certainly be coloured by the political stance of the voter.

It seems safe to assume, however, that in the days before extensive television coverage of politics the influence of party leaders on voting was minimal. For the great mass of voters, their only contact with political leaders was through photographs, newspaper reports of speeches and the occasional radio broadcast. It is instructive to note that the first survey study of voting in Britain (Benney et al. 1956) mentions each party leader only once (and then only to report the number of radio broadcasts they made during the election campaign).

By the 1960s, however, political television was well established and the faces, voices and personalities of party leaders became very familiar to voters. Butler and Stokes (1974) found that the Prime Minister and the Leader of the Opposition were highly visible figures about whom most voters had opinions. To assess the electoral impact of leaders, Butler and Stokes (Ch. 17) compared voters' attitudes to the parties and to the party leaders. They were then able to analyse the voting behaviour of those who were, on balance, favourable to one party but more favourable to the other party's leader. Only relatively small proportions of Butler and Stokes' sample fell into this category — 14 per cent in 1964, 12 per cent in both 1966 and 1970. (The majority of respondents, 55, 64 and 60 per cent respectively, had favourable attitudes to both a party and its leader; the remainder were neutral towards either parties or leaders.)

Among those who favoured one party but another party's leader, it was attitudes to parties that were decisive. Those who were pro-Conservative in terms of attitude to the parties but pro-Labour in their assessment of leaders voted Conservative by three to one; those who were pro-Labour in party terms but pro-Conservative in terms of leaders voted Labour by two to one. None the less, Butler and Stokes do show that party leaders had some impact, especially in the 1970 election. The proportions voting for their favoured party despite preferring the opposing party's leader were much smaller than those supporting their preferred party when they also favoured that party's leader. In addition, when voters were balanced or neutral in their attitudes to the parties but favoured one of the leaders, they tended to vote for that leader's party.

The conclusion reached by Butler and Stokes is judicious. They say that if there is a marked imbalance in the public's estimation of party leaders, if one is clearly preferred or more disliked than another, then that will have some impact on voting choice. This was, indeed, the case in the 1960s when Harold Wilson, the Labour leader, was clearly preferred to Sir Alec Douglas-Home and then to Edward Heath. But even in these cases Butler and Stokes counsel caution. They say that 'the pull of the leaders remains but one among the factors that determine transient shifts of party strength; it is easily outweighed by other issues and events of concern to the public' (p. 368).

Evidence about the impact of party leaders in more recent elections is contained in the series of election commentaries by Ivor Crewe (1981a, 1985b, 1987b). In 1979, when the leaders were James Callaghan (Labour), Margaret Thatcher (Conservative) and David Steel (Liberal), the electorate preferred Mr Callaghan as Prime Minister but the Conservatives won the election. Crewe (1981a, pp. 274−5) explains this apparent paradox in a clear statement of the standard argument about the role of party leaders in British elections:

> The purpose of general elections is not primarily to choose a party leader to become prime minister but to choose a party to form a government. More importantly, the British electorate tends to vote according to what a party represents rather than who represents the party . . . British voters, if forced to choose between leader and party, tend to abandon the leader.

Although Mr Callaghan was popular in 1979, Mrs Thatcher was not very unpopular. When not forced to choose between the two, voters gave Mrs Thatcher good ratings. It seems clear, however, that in this election the impact of the leaders was small.

In 1983 the situation was different. Michael Foot was now Labour leader and he was a significant electoral handicap. Table 5.1 shows which of the party leaders was thought by the voters to be the best person and which the worst person to be Prime Minister. (Steel and Jenkins were joint leaders of the Alliance in this election.)

Only 13 per cent of voters thought that Mr Foot would make the best Prime Minister and 63 per cent thought he would be the worst. Crewe comments: 'Not since the war had a major party leader been regarded as so implausible a prime minister as Michael Foot' (1985b, p. 181). Although Mrs Thatcher was much more popular she was not an unqualified bonus for the Conservatives. Less than half of the voters

Table 5.1 Best and worst person for Prime Minister, 1983

	Best (%)	Worst (%)	Overall score
Thatcher	46	25	+21
Foot	13	63	−50
Steel	35	2	+33
Jenkins	6	10	−4

Source: Crewe (1985a, p. 181).
Note: 'Overall score' is % saying 'best' minus % saying 'worst'.

believed she would make the best Prime Minsiter, and her lead over Mr Steel in this respect was not large. Moreover, during her four years in office Mrs Thatcher had aroused a good deal of hostility among some voters, and a quarter thought she would be the worst person for Prime Minister.

There was a clear connection between these perceptions of the major party leaders and voting choice. Among people who voted Labour in 1979 but did not in 1983, Mr Foot's overall score was −54 and Mrs Thatcher's −8, whereas among those who remained loyal to Labour, Mr Foot scored +34 and Mrs Thatcher −59. Crewe concludes that the party leaders had a negative effect in 1983. Mr Foot, in particular, put people off voting Labour, but hostility to Mrs Thatcher also kept some voters out of the Conservative camp. The lack of positive impact is illustrated by the fact that the popularity enjoyed by Mr Steel (he had the best overall rating) did not enable his party to make a breakthrough.

Comparable figures for the 1987 election are shown in Table 5.2. (By this time Mr Kinnock was Labour leader and Mr Steel and Dr Owen were joint leaders of the Alliance.) Mrs Thatcher had become more unpopular but was still a net electoral asset to the Conservatives. Mr Kinnock was much more popular than Mr Foot had been, but he was still the most 'popular' choice as worst Prime Minister and he had a negative rating overall. The turnaround in Mr Steel's popularity is difficult to explain (but see Chapter 3, note 3). There was, then, a much smaller imbalance in the electorate's assessment of the two major party leaders than in 1983, and to that extent the impact of the leaders was smaller.

This discussion of evidence from the last three elections is far from being an exhaustive analysis of the impact of party leaders. As I sug-

Table 5.2 Best and worst person for Prime Minister, 1987

	Best (%)	Worst (%)	Overall score
Thatcher	42	34	+8
Kinnock	31	44	−13
Steel	10	12	−2
Owen	17	10	+7

Source: Crewe (1987b).
Note: As Table 5.1.

gested earlier, any such analysis would need to try to estimate the electoral effect of leaders independently of such things as party policies and the voter's general political stance, and that is very difficult. It seems, however, that the conclusion reached by Butler and Stokes remains true. Party leaders affect voting behaviour and hence election results only when there is a large difference in how they are regarded by the voters. Even then their impact is muted. To avoid significant electoral damage all that parties have to do is to select a leader who is not patently unpopular or perceived to be lacking in competence.

Election campaigns

In Britain the period of the election campaign is legally defined. It must cover at least three weeks before polling day but is usually four weeks long. It is only during the legally defined campaign period that the various rules regulating candidates' spending, broadcasting and other campaign activities apply. This does not mean that parties campaign only in this period. Far from it. To some extent, parties are campaigning all the time and, certainly in the year before an election is due (the precise date is determined by the Prime Minister), they clearly engage in what is recognisably campaign activity.

During the formal campaign period, however, there is a massive increase in political activity. Media coverage reaches saturation point with the progress of the campaign being charted day by day. The parties and the politicians expend vast amounts of money and effort in trying to win votes. In the 1987 election, the three major parties spent about £15 million centrally and another £7.5 million in the constituencies (Butler and Kavanagh 1988, p. 235). In addition they received free time for election broadcasts on television and radio, and a free postal delivery to every elector.

Does all of this have any effect? Do campaigns swing votes or are they three weeks of 'sound and fury, signifying nothing'?[1] As before, the shift from aligned to dealigned voting provides a framework within which the effects of campaigns can be evaluated.

With aligned voting, the election campaign is merely one other short-term factor which might marginally affect the voters. Since most voters had enduring party loyalties they were unlikely to be deflected from them by any incidents occurring in a short campaign. Compared to the deep-seated influences of class and party identification, campaigns paled into insignificance. As these enduring ties have loosened, however, it seems possible that voters have become more open to influence during campaigns. Fewer will have their minds already made up when the campaign begins.

Some support for this interpretation is given in Table 5.3. The first row of the table shows the percentages of voters who claimed that they made up their minds about which party to support during the campaign itself. Although changes in the wording of the question used to obtain this information in different surveys complicate interpretation, it is clear that the figures from 1974 onwards are much larger than previously. The second row shows the percentages who said that they had seriously considered voting for a party other than the one they finally chose. Again, changes in question wording complicate matters but, although the trend here is less clear, the highest figures were recorded in 1979 and 1987.

Thus far, I have discussed election campaigns in a general way. For more detailed consideration we need to distinguish two levels of campaigning. On the one hand there are local campaigns. In every constituency candidates and party workers put up posters, deliver leaflets, canvass voters, hold meetings, make statements to the local press and try to get their supporters to the polls on election day. Ordinary voters have direct contact with the campaign at this level. On the other hand there is the national campaign. This is dominated by the party leaderships, with daily press conferences, walkabouts, set-piece addresses to party rallies, election broadcasts and TV interviews. Overwhelmingly, the voters experience this campaign only through the mass media, especially television.

Table 5.3 Late deciders and waverers, 1964—87 (%)

	1964	1966	1970	Feb. 1974	Oct. 1974	1979	1983	1987
Late deciders	12	11	12	23	22	28	22	21
Waverers	24	22	21	25	21	31	25	27

Source: Heath *et al.* (1988). Quoted with permission.
Note: 'Late deciders' refers to the percentage of voters who reported that they made their minds up about which party to support during the campaign itself. 'Waverers' refers to the percentage who seriously considered voting for a party other than the one they finally chose.

Local campaigns

In the 1950s and 1960s, whether they knew it or not, the local campaigning techniques adopted by the political parties were based on an acceptance of the model of stable voting which I outlined in Chapter 2. The main purpose of the campaign was to identify known or likely supporters and ensure that they voted. Each party knew where its supporters were to be found — in council estates and other working-class areas for Labour, in private housing estates and middle-class suburbs for the Tories — and concentrated their attention there. Party workers were actively discouraged from 'wasting time' by trying to persuade opponents or 'doubtful' voters of the merits of their candidate. The underlying assumption was that party loyalties were more or less fixed and the aim of the campaign was to maximise the turnout of supporters.

Constituency campaigns were not primarily intended, therefore, to alter the party choice of electors, although they were intended to influence the result of an election. Even in this limited respect, however, there is little evidence that constituency campaigns made a difference. In local government elections effective campaigning could have a significant impact (see Bochel and Denver 1971), but the consensus is that in general elections, apart from rare special cases, local campaigning could affect the election outcome only if there was an enormous difference in the organisational effectiveness of the contending parties, and even then the effect was slight.

Today, voters continue to have direct contact with general election campaigns at local level. In the 1987 election 92 per cent of voters reported that they received election leaflets through the door, 49 per cent that they had been canvassed, 46 per cent that they had seen election advertisements on hoardings and 16 per cent that they had been contacted on election day itself (Butler and Kavanagh 1988, pp. 214–5). Attendance at public meetings, once an important feature of election campaigns, is now minimal, however, with only 3 per cent of electors reporting attending a meeting in 1987 — and most of these would be the party faithful turning out to support their candidate.

There is some indirect evidence that local campaigning nowadays may have a greater effect than before upon the voters. It is now fairly common, for example, for there to be massive turnovers of opinion in parliamentary by-elections. But by-elections are atypical in that parties devote great resources to them — bringing in national officials as organisers and party workers from near and far — and the media bring the full glare of national publicity on to an individual constituency in a way that is not possible in a general election. General election results themselves, however, have shown an increasing variablity in results from constituency to constituency (see Chapter 6). More individual candidates are able to buck the national trend and it may be that this is a product of local campaigning. In addition, recent elections have seen a good deal of 'tactical' voting in some constituencies. That is, significant numbers of voters have opted for their second-choice party in order to defeat their least-favoured party. Where this happens, local party organisations must play an important part in informing voters of the tactical situation in the constituency and in persuading them of the potential effectiveness of a tactical vote.

None the less, this evidence is fragmentary and the arguments are largely speculative. Such more direct evidence as is available tends to confirm the established view that local campaigning has little effect. Crewe (1981a, p. 272) reports that in 1979 3 per cent of voters said that their vote was affected by being canvassed by a party worker and 2 per cent said they were affected by seeing campaign posters. Similarly small percentages of voters made the same claim in 1983. As Crewe notes, the likelihood is that many of those claiming to have been influenced would have voted for the party of their choice in any case, so that the real impact of local campaigns is probably minimal.

Localised campaigning has many functions. It gives local parties a sense of purpose, gives party workers the satisfaction of extensive involvement in the electoral process, and allows candidates the opportunity to meet the public. Except in unusual circumstances, however, it does not greatly affect the decisions of voters.

The national campaign

Elections used to be much less 'general' than they are now. In the nineteenth and early twentieth centuries a 'general' election was really a series of individual constituency contests with little central involvement or direction. It was not until 1918 that all constituencies polled on the same day.

The growth of the mass media has changed all this. Elections are now nationwide contests and the national campaign is the dominant focus of attention. Modern campaigns are media campaigns; they are a form of spectator sport. Most people do not participate in them but watch them on television or read about them in the newspapers. As has often been observed, a party leader making an election broadcast today will talk

Table 5.4 Sources of political information, 1983 (%)

	Most important source	Top two most important sources
Television	63	88
Newspapers	29	73
Radio	4	14
Personal contacts	3	12
Other	1	3

Source: Dunleavy and Husbands (1985, p. 11).

to more people in 10 minutes than Gladstone and Disraeli did together throughout their careers.

Since the 1960s television has utterly dominated national campaigns. The activities of the party leaders are 'media events' especially staged to be reported; 'photo opportunities' are carefully arranged; schedules are timed to fit in with television news coverage. When leading politicians address meetings they do not really speak to their live audiences — who are occasionally glimpsed glassy-eyed with incomprehension — but to the TV audience who will see clips from the speech ('sound bites' is the American expression) later in the evening.

The extent to which electors follow elections via the media is clear. In 1987, 75 per cent of voters reported that they had seen a party election broadcast (Butler and Kavanagh 1988, p. 215) and almost everyone must have seen some campaign coverage. Table 5.4 shows that television is said by voters to be their most important source of political information, with newspapers being an important secondary source.

The distinction to be made between the national election campaign and media coverage of the campaign has become increasingly blurred. To all intents and purposes, examining the impact of the national campaign is the same as examining the impact of the mass media upon the voters during the campaign.

The effects of the media

The question of the extent to which people's attitudes, opinions and behaviour are influenced by the mass media, especially television, is one that has provoked an enormous amount of research.

Early media theorists, impressed by the apparent power of the media to influence ideas, posited what is called a *direct-effects* or *hypodermic-needle* model. This is illustrated in Figure 5.1. The source or sender (S) communicates information by a particular channel (print or television) to a receiver (R). The receiver receives the message directly, accepts it and is influenced by it.

Empirical research on political attitudes quickly found that this model was far too simplistic (see Trenaman and McQuail 1961; Blumler and McQuail 1967). Voters did not come to political television in a vacuum, as it were. Rather, they already had opinions, values and experiences which affected their perceptions and interpretations of media messages. The direct-effects model was, therefore, replaced by the *filter* model, which is illustrated in Figure 5.2.

An important psychological theory underlies this model — the theory of *cognitive dissonance*. Cognitive dissonance is a psychological state of unease or tension which occurs when an individual encounters facts or arguments that are at variance with his or her beliefs or attitudes. Subconsciously everyone wants to avoid this, and does so by 'screening out' some information while being receptive to other information. Generally, people seek reinforcement of their own position from the media, and seek to avoid communications which contradict their views. This is done in three ways:

(1) Selective exposure. We cannot read all the newspapers or watch all television programmes. We tend to read and watch material that supports our political viewpoint, for example. Indeed, many people avoid

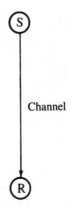

Figure 5.1 Direct-effects model of media influence

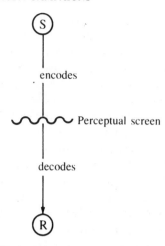

Figure 5.2 Filter model of media influence

'political' material altogether and concentrate on sport, entertainment, 'Page 3 girls' and so on.

(2) Selective perception. Even when we come across hostile media material, we reinterpret it to fit in with our preconceptions or do not even perceive its hostility. As Simon and Garfunkel put it a long time ago in a popular song, 'A man hears what he wants to hear and disregards the rest.'

(3) Selective retention. We remember selectively. We remember things that fit in with our views and quickly forget things that do not.

People employ these mechanisms subconsciously in 'decoding' the communications that have been 'encoded' by the sender. In doing so they erect a 'communications barrier' or 'perceptual screen' between themselves and the mass media. Despite all the propaganda efforts of the newspapers and of the parties in campaign broadcasts, the main effect of the media as interpreted by this model is to reinforce the voters' predispositions.

The press

This thesis is well illustrated by analysis of the role of the press in influencing political attitudes. The national press in Britain is overwhelmingly and clearly partisan. On election day in February 1974, for example, the whole of the front page of the *Daily Mirror* was taken up with the slogan, 'FOR ALL OUR TOMORROWS VOTE LABOUR TODAY'. It would be difficult to be more clearly partisan than that! But few readers of this book would have any difficulty in saying which party is supported by each national newspaper. Table 5.5 shows how the papers lined up at the 1987 general election.

There is clearly a strong pro-Conservative bias in national daily newspapers. The circulation of pro-Conservative papers totals 10.4 millions: all the rest total only 4.2 millions. From time to time people point to this discrepancy (especially at Labour party conferences) and claim that it accounts for the poor showing of Labour and for Conservative dominance in recent elections. But this is to make a too-simple connection between what the papers say and what the voters do.

It is certainly the case that there is a correlation between the papers people read and the party they vote for. Table 5.6 shows the vote of the readers of the various papers in 1987. The relationship is far from perfect — only a minority of the readers of the extravagantly pro-Conservative *Sun* actually votes Conservative, for example — but it is fairly consistent and clear. What is not clear, however, is how these data are to be interpreted. It is not clear whether readers' political views are shaped by the paper they read or whether they choose a paper which is politically congenial to them. In other words, the data may reflect selective exposure.

In the 1960s Butler and Stokes (1974) found similar relationships between newspaper reading habits and party choice. They concluded, however, that in general the relationship was a spurious one:

> The correlation is most likely to have been produced by the family's passing on a partisanship which the child has matched by his choice of paper,

Table 5.5 Partisanship of the national daily press, 1987

Conservative		Labour	
Sun	(4.0)	Daily Mirror	(3.1)
Daily Mail	(1.8)	*Anti-Conservative*	
Daily Express	(1.7)	Guardian	(0.5)
Daily Star	(1.3)	Today	(0.3)
Daily Telegraph	(1.2)	*None*	
The Times	(0.4)	Independent	(0.3)

Source: Butler and Kavanagh (1988, pp. 165–6).
Note: Circulation figures (in millions) are shown in brackets.

Table 5.6 Party choice by newspaper read, 1987 (%)

	Vote of readers		
	Conservative	Labour	Alliance
Sun	41	31	19
Daily Mail	60	13	19
Daily Express	70	9	18
Daily Star	28	46	18
Daily Telegraph	80	5	10
The Times	56	12	27
Daily Mirror	20	55	21
Guardian	22	54	19
Today	43	17	40
Independent	34	34	27

Source: Butler and Kavanagh (1988, p. 187).
Note: No figures are given for *Financial Times* in the original.

or by its passing on a more general social location to which both paper and party are appropriate . . . it is clear that newspapers often profit from, rather than shape, their reader's party ties (p. 118).

None the less, Butler and Stokes emphasise that the press plays a part in conserving or reinforcing party loyalties. Also, it has a minor role in creating a party preference where readers were previously uncommitted.

A similarly careful analysis of the political effects of reading different newspapers in 1983 is given by Martin Harrop (1986). He too finds some support for the view that papers can help to shape a party preference where readers previously had none, but he concludes that the main effect of the press is the reinforcement of existing party loyalties. He finds no consistent evidence that newspapers convert their readers to the party supported by the paper.

This view represents the consensus among political scientists on the role of the press in influencing voting behaviour. A dissenting view is held by Dunleavy and Husbands (1985, pp. 110–17). They take account of the fact that many people read more than one newspaper (including Sunday papers) and argue that even when occupational class is taken into account there are clear differences in party choice between voters which reflect the predominant partisan stance of the newspapers that they read. Unfortunately the number of respondents in some of the categories used by Dunleavy and Husbands in their analysis is very small indeed, and they fail to deal adequately with the problem of selective exposure. Their only comment on the latter is: 'The relationship we have traced seems too close to be attributable solely or even mainly to partisan self-selection into readership' (p. 114). Of course, partisan self-selection would be *expected* to produce a very close relationship.

The weight of the evidence suggests, then, that voters tend to use the press rather as the filter model would predict. There is a good deal of selective exposure, and in 'decoding' media messages most voters appear to seek reinforcement for their political positions. The ability of newspapers to convert, to swing votes, is very limited. This is not to say that the press has no influence at all during the campaigns. As Harrop notes, newspapers often initiate discussion on campaign issues and events which are then picked up by television commentators and conveyed to a mass audience. The press, in other words, helps to set the campaign agenda.

Television

Unlike the press, television coverage of politics is avowedly non-partisan (except, of course, for party political broadcasts). The BBC and the independent television companies are legally obliged to maintain neutrality between parties and great efforts are made by them to ensure that the major parties receive equal amounts of coverage. Television, as we have seen, is a much more important means of political communication than the press and it now dominates election campaigns. To be a successful party leader these days it is important to 'come over' well on television.

The two pioneering studies of the effects of television on British voting behaviour (Trenaman and McQuail 1961; Blumler and McQuail 1967) found that among a variety of sources of political information only television was able to overcome the 'communications barrier' between people and the media. But it did so only to the extent of increasing the voters' level of political information. It did not change but rather reinforced political attitudes and opinions. The two books provide clear support for the filter model of media effects. Thus, Trenaman and McQuail conclude that 'In the field of attitudes a highly significant screening effect separates exposure to the campaign from changes in strength or direction of attitude' (p. 233). They say that there is 'a definite and consistent barrier between source of communication and movement of attitudes in the political field at the General Election' (p. 192).

Many people find the conclusion that television has little effect on political opinions difficult to accept. It seems to fly in the face of common sense to suggest that such a pervasive medium has little impact upon political attitudes and behaviour. I myself have pointed to increased coverage of politics on television as a source of dealignment (Chapter 3). Moreover, if television has such little impact upon voters why do the professionals in the political parties assiduously tailor their campaigns to television?

In attempting to resolve this paradox one preliminary point needs to be made. Both of the studies mentioned — and many others besides — were conducted in situations in which all parties had access to television. Their authors would not deny that if one party had a monopoly, or even a disproportionately large share of television coverage, then the results could be quite different. Parties could not, on the basis of these research findings, simply opt out of campaigning via television and leave the field free to their opponents.

It is also important to remember that both of the studies referred to were completed more than 20 years ago. Trenaman and McQuail's book is concerned with the 1959 general election while Blumler and McQuail's deals with the 1964 election. Much has changed since then. The quantity of political coverage on television has greatly increased and its quality has vastly improved: television commentators, interviewers and presenters concerned with political coverage are much more professional.

Among voters, the change from aligned to dealigned voting has serious implications for the filter model. It was the existence of party identification which strengthened the communications barrier. It was because most voters had strong pre-existing party loyalties that they employed selective processes in response to political messages in the media. If people were strongly Conservative they would screen out pro-Labour information and remember pro-Conservative information. We have seen, however, that there has been a notable decline in the strength of party identification and it would, therefore, seem reasonable to infer that the communications barrier has become rather more permeable.

Another change has been in the party system. When these studies were undertaken, the supremacy of the Conservative and Labour parties was virtually unchallenged. Today, the system is more complex and it is relevant to note that Blumler and McQuail (Ch. 11) suggest that a general effect of election broadcasting might be to improve the position of third parties.

A major problem with both studies is that their focus is very much short term. They concentrate on the election campaign period only and on changes in voting intentions and attitudes (rather than, for example, reinforcement or crystallisation). The main reason for their short-term focus is that it is difficult (and expensive) to construct a research programme to study the long-term effects of television. Indeed, it is difficult even to imagine how this could be done since people are constantly exposed to a multiplicity of other influences. None the less, it seems unrealistic to expect to find marked changes in political opinions in such a short space of time, especially in a situation where voting was highly structured by class and party identification. Television's influence could be long term, slow and subtle — but none the less real. Party election broadcasts might not convert people but that does not mean that attitudes might not be shaped over a long period.

This argument has been put forward in a series of studies by the Glasgow University Media Group (1976, 1980, 1982). These researchers analysed the output of television news broadcasts and concluded that TV news is not neutral in its treatment of stories but displays a consistent bias against left-wing political views. News is reported from a vaguely middle-of-the-road perspective. However, the Glasgow group's concentration upon the *output* of television means that they do not study with any seriousness the *effects* on viewers' opinions of the bias they allege. In addition, the methodology and conclusions of these studies have been severely criticised (see Harrison 1985).

There has been no full-scale study of the effects of television upon voting behaviour in the period of dealignment. Simple observation suggests, however, that television now plays a bigger role in campaigns. In particular, its role as agenda-setter is clear. It is television producers and commentators who decide which campaign issues will be discussed and which events reported. Party spokesmen in TV interviews try hard to talk about the issues *they* want to publicise (usually because they know that these are issues on which the electorate are favourable to their party) but interviewers often relentlessly pursue the topics that *they* think the viewers want to hear about.

The conditions for increased television influence exist. Party identification, which previously filtered voters' perceptions of political communications, has declined in importance. Issue voting has become more prevalent and a precondition of issue voting is information. Television is by far the main supplier of political information. Furthermore, if voters are affected by the personalities and performance of party leaders, this must largely be based on the image projected by leaders on television.

It may be, however, that the influence of television is so pervasive, long-term and mixed up with other factors that it is simply beyond the current ability of social science methods to measure it empirically.

Public opinion polls

Public opinion polls are now a familiar part of general election campaigns. They are closely related to media campaign coverage, since it is newspapers and television programmes which commission many of the polls, and the voters read and hear about polls in the press and on television. In recent years the number of published campaign polls has increased dramatically. Table 5.7 shows the number of nationwide polls published during the campaign period in elections since 1970. It should be noted that in addition to the 54 separate nationwide polls reported in the table for the 1987 election there were also 18 reports of a 'rolling poll' by TV AM and at least 100 other polls covering individual constituencies, groups of marginal seats and particular areas such as Scotland and the North West. All of this activity made 1987 'by a considerable margin, the most exhaustively polled election in British history' (Butler and Kavanagh 1988, p. 124). Even so, at the end of the campaign only two-thirds of voters could recall seeing or hearing about a poll result, which was about the same proportion as in 1983 (Gallup 1987; Rose 1985).

Although a number of smaller companies are involved, political polling in Britain is dominated by five major firms. These are Gallup (the

Table 5.7 Number of nationwide campaign polls published

1970	Feb. 1974	Oct. 1974	1979	1983	1987
25	25	27	26	49	54

Sources: Butler and Pinto-Duschinsky (1971, p. 178); Butler and Kavanagh (1974, p. 95; 1975, pp. 190–1; 1980, p. 264; 1984, p. 124; 1988, p. 138).

oldest), National Opinion Polls (NOP), Marplan, Harris, and Market and Opinion Research International (MORI). These are highly reputable companies and it would be very much against their interests if any of their clients were to distort their results. There is no question of the media 'fiddling' poll figures. What the polling firms cannot control, however, is editorial comment or newspaper headlines and sometimes these give a misleading impression of what a poll has actually found.

Campaign poll results are sometimes portrayed as predictions of the outcome of the election in question. Strictly speaking, this is a misunderstanding. What campaign polls actually provide is a snapshot of the electorate's voting intentions at a particular point in time, not a prediction of how they will vote at a later date. ('Exit' polls are not strictly campaign polls and their purpose clearly *is* predictive.) None the less, the polling firms themselves treat their final polls as forecasts of the election result, and the accuracy of polls is often assessed by comparing the result of the final poll produced by each company with the actual election result. The accuracy of the polls in recent elections in this respect is summarised in Table 5.8.[2]

Overall, the record is very creditable, especially when it is borne in mind that not everyone questioned by pollsters actually votes in the election. In addition, given dealigned voting, polling firms now have to cope with more 'late deciders' and 'waverers' as well as a more fragmented party system. There is, too, always the possibility that the polls may be self-falsifying, since the publication of their results may alter the very behaviour that they are trying to describe.

Finally it should be noted that what polls attempt to measure is the distribution of party support among the electorate. Extrapolating from this to the distribution of seats in the House of Commons is a tricky business which is becoming trickier. In February 1974, for example, the party which won most votes (the Conservatives) did not win most

Table 5.8 Average error per party in final campaign polls

1964	1966	1970	Feb. 1974	Oct. 1974	1979	1983	1987
1.3	1.7	2.6	2.2	2.2	1.0	1.7	1.6
(4)	(4)	(5)	(6)	(4)	(5)	(7)	(6)

Sources: Rose (1985, p. 132); Butler and Kavanagh (1988, p. 132).
Note: Figures in brackets indicate the number of final polls.

seats. In 1987 ITN seriously underestimated the likely Conservative majority in the House of Commons despite the fact that its exit poll, conducted by Harris, got the Conservative lead over Labour in terms of vote share almost exactly right.

Does the publication of opinion poll results influence voting behaviour? Despite the reference above to the possibility of self-falsification, the answer to this evergreen question about the polls is, at a general level, 'No'. There have been two main hypotheses in this area — the 'band-wagon' effect and the 'boomerang' effect. The first suggests that when one party is seen to be in the lead some voters will 'jump on the band-wagon' and its support will increase, while supporters of the losing party will lose heart and may not vote. The 'boomerang' hypothesis says exactly the opposite: supporters of the leading party become complacent, and sympathy for the underdog results in an upsurge of support for the trailing party. Clearly, both hypotheses cannot be true but in fact neither is. There is no consistent pattern which supports either hypothesis (see Teer and Spence 1973, Ch. 6).

It is possible that third-party support is influenced by poll results. During the 1983 campaign, Alliance support improved rapidly as polling day approached. Alliance-inclined voters, it could be argued, were encouraged by the first signs of improvement in the polls and switched to the Alliance, thereby producing a sort of 'multiplier' effect. Alliance leaders were, indeed, accused by their opponents of 'talking up' their level of support in the polls in order to achieve just such an effect. After the election, Gallup found that among voters who had seen the results of a poll, 9 per cent of Alliance voters said that their vote had been influenced by the polls, compared with only 2 per cent and 3 per cent of Conservative and Labour voters respectively (Rose 1985, p. 131). In contrast, during the 1987 campaign the Alliance failed to register any significant increase in support until the very end of the campaign, and this may have dissuaded some potential supporters from voting for them. In both of these cases, however, it is impossible to know whether the polls were creating an effect or merely reflecting what was happening, quite independently, among the electorate. Moreover, no 'multiplier' effect appeared in February 1974, when polls later in the campaign consistently *overestimated* Liberal support.

Another way in which opinion poll results might influence voting has come to prominence in recent years. This is the role polls can have in assisting tactical voting. A particularly striking example of this occurred in a by-election in Bermondsey in February 1983. This had formerly been a very safe Labour seat but the Labour candidate in the by-election was highly unpopular and a majority of the electorate did not want to vote for him. There were, however, two other candidates who were thought to be in a position to challenge for the seat — an Alliance candidate and a local 'Real Labour' candidate. On the Friday before the election, an NOP poll was published in the *Daily Mail* showing support for the parties as Labour 37 per cent, Alliance 25 per cent, Real Labour 24 per cent and Conservatives 11 per cent. Despite the statistical insignificance of the difference between the Alliance and Real Labour, the poll was widely interpreted as showing that the Alliance was in second place. On the following Tuesday, Thames Television announced the results of a poll by Opinion Research Centre which showed Labour and the Alliance neck and neck at 30 per cent each, followed by Real Labour on 16 per cent and the Conservatives on 10 per cent. These results were 'splashed' in the popular press. The election took place on the Thursday and the result was Alliance 58 per cent, Labour 26 per cent, Real Labour 8 per cent and Conservatives 6 per cent. Although the Labour candidate lost support as the campaign progressed, the most striking development in voting intention is the massive shift from Real Labour and the Conservatives to the Alliance, and it was widely claimed that the publication of the poll results decisively influenced the eventual outcome of the by-election.

It is important to note, however, that this example concerns polls in a single constituency at a by-election. Since tactical voting in the sense used here is essentially a constituency-level matter, there is no straightforward way in which national opinion polls in a general election could be used as the basis for tactical voting. Moreover, no constituency in a general election is the subject of the intense publicity and campaign activity that occurs in by-elections; there are relatively few single-constituency polls. Even when these are undertaken, their impact is much smaller. There is no evidence that the single-constituency polls which were published during the 1987 election campaign had any systematic and significant impact on the results. Even in the Bermondsey case it is not clear that we should talk of the polls 'influencing' voters. Rather, it might be claimed that the polls merely provided neutral information which voters could take account of, if they so wished, in order to use their vote more effectively to achieve their desired outcome.

There are, then, few grounds for believing that public opinion polls directly influence voters. This is not to say that they are not an important aspect of election campaigns. The political parties closely monitor the polls and themselves employ firms to do private polls for them. They build their campaign strategies around what the polls tell them. It is well documented, for example, that on Thursday, 4 June 1987 ('Wobbly Thursday'), the Conservative campaign organisation was afflicted by a severe crisis of confidence when a couple of polls appeared to suggest some slippage in Conservative support (see Butler and Kavanagh 1988, pp. 107−11). The media also frequently use poll results as the centrepiece of their election coverage. The higher profile of polls in campaigns should not be confused, however, with their ability to influence voters.

It is often argued that the publication of opinion poll results should be banned during election campaigns in Britain, as it is in some other countries. The Speaker's Conference on Electoral Reform recommended this in 1967 but the proposal was not accepted by the government. None the less, the issue continues to be raised. Those who favour banning them believe that polls do affect voting behaviour, and also argue that they 'trivialise' elections by reducing them to 'horse races' and deflecting the attention of the voters from the serious issues at stake (see Whiteley 1986).

If the publication of polls were banned, however, they would merely be replaced by leaks from private polls, rumour and deliberate disinformation campaigns. Local parties and candidates are not above referring to 'polls' of doubtful validity, or even inventing 'poll' results in their campaign literature. We are all familiar with the campaign organiser who claims that canvass returns show that his party is doing 'very well' and support is 'holding up', when the election result turns out to be a disaster. It seems better, on the whole, to have polls by firms with no political axe to grind.

More positively, reliable information about the relative support for parties is something that voters may wish to take into account before deciding how to vote. And why should they be denied it? Opinion polls by reputable companies can be counted as a benefit to the electoral process, not as a problem.

Campaign trends in voting intentions

The data presented in Table 5.3 showed evidence of increased indecision among voters about which party to support during recent election campaigns. The extent to which this is reflected in changes in aggregate voting intentions is illustrated in Figures 5.3 and 5.4.

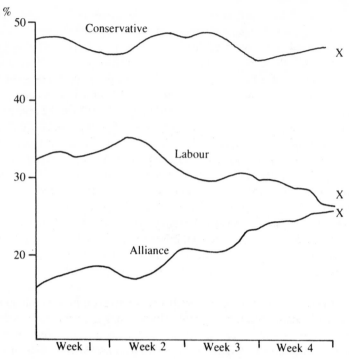

Note: The graph represents the daily 'moving average' percentage for each party and is based on polls produced by the five major companies mentioned in the text. The actual share of votes received is indicated by 'X'.

Figure 5.3 Trends in voting intentions during the campaign, 1983

Figure 5.3 shows trends in voting intentions during the 1983 general election campaign. Evidence of opinion change in the course of a campaign could hardly be clearer. During the last two and a half weeks of the campaign there was a steady decline in support for Labour and an increase in Alliance support, to the extent that they almost snatched second place, despite having started the campaign well behind. It seems clear that the campaign importantly affected the final outcome.

The trend in the 1987 election was very different (Figure 5.4). In this case there was an initial settling down but then, for the last three weeks of the campaign, there was very little movement. It must be remembered, however, that the graph summarises the net effect of individual changes. During this campaign, a study was carried out in which the voting intentions of a panel of individual voters were tracked (Miller et al. 1988).

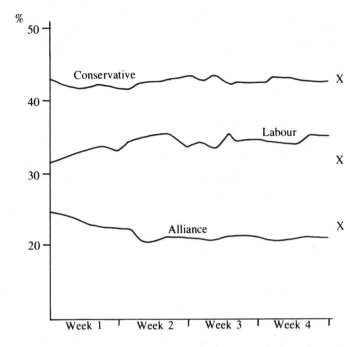

Note: As Figure 5.3.

Figure 5.4 Trends in voting intentions during the campaign, 1987

This found that 13 per cent of the voters eventually chose a party different from the one they were most inclined to support at the outset of the campaign, and a further 8 per cent moved from a position of having no preference to support for one party or another. There was, then, quite considerable individual change during the campaign but these changes tended to cancel out so that they did not have a major impact on the aggregate trend.

We can conclude from our discussion of campaign effects that, as compared with 20 years ago, election campaigns are now, potentially, more likely to influence voters and election outcomes. The dealigned electorate is more open to persuasion. If a party has a disastrous campaign or commits serious gaffes (as Labour did in 1983), the election result will be importantly affected. If, however, all parties run careful, professional campaigns, the short-term instability among the voters will not be markedly to the benefit or disadvantage of any one of the parties. It is important, then, for a party to have good campaigns. The apparent lack of effect in 1987 is deceptive — as any party which did not campaign seriously and well would soon find out.

Notes

1. The quotation is used as the title of an article on the 1987 campaign by Pippa Norris (1987). The allusion is, of course, to *Macbeth* Act V, Scene v.
2. The figure for each election is the mean of the differences between the share of the votes obtained by each of the three major parties and the average share of the vote forecast for each in final campaign polls.

6

Trends in British General Elections

In previous chapters I have been mainly concerned with survey evidence about voting behaviour in Britain. The focus has been on individual electors. In this chapter I turn to election results themselves — the aggregate effect of the voting decisions made by individuals. There is an obvious link between individual behaviour and election results: we would expect that the developments in voting behaviour at the individual level which I have considered would be reflected at the aggregate level.

The study of election results has a lengthy tradition in Britain, predating the emergence of survey studies. After every election since 1945 a volume has been published (entitled *The British General Election of . . .*) providing an account of the election campaign and analysis of the results. The books are known as the 'Nuffield studies' because of their connection with Nuffield College, Oxford and, except for the first two, every one has been authored or co-authored by David Butler.

Any election contested by political parties provides two pieces of information which constitute the basic dependent variables in the analysis of election results — the number of eligible electors who vote (turnout) and the distribution of votes among the competing parties. (Other information such as the number of spoiled ballot papers, the sex of candidates and the position of candidates on the ballot paper can also usually be obtained and used in analysis.) In a single general election, we have this information for 650 constituencies[1] and we can analyse variations in the dependent variables across constituencies. This is called *cross-sectional* analysis. When more than one election or a series is studied, we can also analyse change in the variables from one election to another. This is sometimes called *longitudinal* or *time-series* analysis.

Turnout

Turnout in British general elections varies both over time and across constituencies. The national turnout since 1950 is shown in Table 6.1. The figures appear to indicate a downward trend but this is rather misleading. The turnouts in 1950 and 1951 were quite exceptional — from 1922 to 1945 the average turnout was 74 per cent — and if these two are omitted any downward trend is very slight indeed. Moreover, the figures are not directly comparable over the period. In 1970 the voting age was lowered from 21 to 18 and this increased the total electorate by more than three millions as compared with 1966.

In an international context, it is worth noting that British turnout is not particularly high. In a comparative study of turnout, Crewe reports that Britain comes fourteenth out of 20 democracies in terms of turnout in the post-war period (see Crewe 1981b, pp. 234—6).

Even so, it can be argued that turnout in Britain is surprisingly high. Since most seats are 'safe' for one party or another, most electors know who is going to win their seat before they go to vote. In some respects voting is clearly an irrational act. It involves the individual voter in some costs — getting to the polls, for example — and the chances of an individual's vote making any difference to a constituency result, let alone the result of the election as a whole, are infinitesimal. None the less, most electors do turn out in general elections. Voting is widely believed to be a duty of citizens, and the costs involved are so small that they

Table 6.1   Turnout in general elections, 1950—87 (%)

1950	84.0	1970	72.0
1951	82.5	Feb. 1974	78.1
1955	76.8	Oct. 1974	72.8
1959	78.7	1979	76.0
1964	77.1	1983	72.7
1966	75.8	1987	75.3

Source: Butler and Kavanagh (1988, p. 283).

do not deter on the scale that 'pure' rational choice theory would predict (see McLean 1982, Ch. 4).

The comparative point made above raises an important question. What exactly do turnout figures measure? Different countries have different rules about voting — in Australia it is compulsory, for example — and this affects the interpretation of the figures. In Britain, what is measured is the percentage of people whose names are on the electoral register who put a ballot paper into the ballot box. Compiling the electoral register is the responsibility of local authorities. The list is drawn up every October, usually on the basis of information supplied to the local authority on forms which are distributed to every household, institution or other place where voters might live. Although it is drawn up in October, the register does not come into force until the following February and then it lasts for one year.

Even when it is first compiled the register cannot possibly be 100 per cent accurate. People are accidentally missed off (most commonly young people who will become 18 before the register lapses); others are included who should not be; yet others are registered in two places (students, for example, are often registered at their homes and at their college or university). When it comes into force the register is already four months out of date — people will have died, moved or emigrated — and it continues to decay during the year for which it is in force. Official turnout figures do not take account of the accuracy of the electoral register but some electoral analysts have done. Rose (1974, p. 494), for example, calculates that the 'real' turnout figure is obtained by the following formula:

$$\frac{\text{Reported percentage turnout}}{(100+3.4-1.0-0.15m-0.67m)}$$

In this formula, m is the number of months from the compilation of the register to the election; 3.4 is added and 1.0 deducted to take account of electors registered twice and citizens not registered respectively; subtracting $0.15m$ and $0.67m$ adjusts for electors who have died and those who have moved.

National turnout trends taking account of these adjustments are shown in Table 6.2. The impression given by these data is not one of a gentle decline but of a fairly sharp break between 1964 and 1966. Until 1964 turnout easily exceeded 80 per cent in four out of five elections (and the fifth was very close to 80 per cent). From 1966 onwards (and that was before 18-year-olds were given the vote), turnout has regularly been

Table 6.2   Adjusted turnout in general elections, 1950–87 (%)

1950	84.1		1970	75.2
1951	88.3	Feb. 1974	78.8
1955	79.8	Oct. 1974	78.6
1959	85.0		1979	78.6
1964	83.3		1983	75.8
1966	77.4		1987	78.6

Note: Adjustments are made according to the formula described in the text.

in the mid-to-high seventies. I shall return to this difference between the two periods below.

Turnout variation from constituency to constituency is very large. In the 1987 election it ranged from 84.4 per cent (Brecon and Radnor) to 55.4 per cent (Hackney South and Shoreditch). Just under 11 per cent of seats had a turnout above 80 per cent and in 10 per cent of seats the turnout was less than 70 per cent. Clearly, variations such as this require explanation.

Investigations of variations in constituency turnouts have emphasised three main sorts of explanatory factor — social, political and what, for want of a better term, might be called 'cultural'. The normal method of analysis used to investigate the problem is to try to explain variation in the dependent variable (constituency turnout) by reference to a series of independent variables, employing correlation and regression techniques.

As an example of social influences upon turnout, Table 6.3 shows the correlations between four occupational and housing variables and turnout in five general elections between 1964 and 1979. The figures show,

Table 6.3   Correlations between the occupational and housing make-up of constituencies and turnout, 1964–79

	1964	1966	1970	Oct. 1974	1979
% professional and managerial	0.29	0.38	0.29	0.36	0.37
% non-manual	0.17	0.29	0.13	0.17	0.20
% owner-occupiers	0.56	0.59	0.53	0.57	0.58
% council tenants	−0.02	−0.11	−0.05	−0.13	−0.17

Source: Denver and Hands (1985, p. 384).

firstly, that there is a positive relationship between % professional and managerial and turnout, although the coefficients are not very large. That is, the more people there are in a constituency with professional or managerial occupations, the higher tends to be the turnout. On the other hand, the broader middle-class category, % non-manual, is rather weakly related to turnout. The best social predictor of turnout of those shown in the table is % owner-occupiers while % council tenants has a weak negative effect.

It must be stressed that these correlations refer to aggregate data. They refer to the characteristics of constituencies, not individuals. We cannot infer from them that owner-occupiers turn out in greater numbers than other people. Rather the figures tell us that the greater the proportion of owner-occupiers in a constituency the higher, usually, is the turnout. The reason for this may be that high levels of owner-occupation are associated with stable, settled communities and, in these, the norm of voting in elections is well established. Support for this interpretation is provided by a forthcoming study of turnout (Eagles and Erfle 1989) in which the authors devised some ingenious measures of 'community cohesion' and found that it was positively correlated with general election turnout.

The correlations between turnout and two 'political' factors are shown in Table 6.4. It might be expected that multiparty contests would generate more interest among electors, especially when there is considerable support for a third party, and lead to higher levels of turnout. When we test this, however, we find that the correlations between the share of the vote gained by third and other parties and constituency turnout are erratic and declined markedly in the 1970s, when 'minor' party candidates became more common.

The opposite is true of 'marginality', or the closeness of the contest in the previous election. This is an important and increasingly significant predictor of constituency turnout (see also Eagles and Erfle 1989;

Table 6.4 Correlations between minor-party support, marginality and turnout, 1964—79

	1964	1966	1970	Oct. 1974	1979
% minor party	0.31	0.27	0.37	0.29	0.18
Marginality	0.23	0.46	0.44	0.48	0.51

Source: Denver and Hands (1985, pp. 382—4).

Mughan 1986). I have shown (Denver and Hands, 1974, 1985) that even when a variety of other social and political variables are taken into account marginality remains important. In our first report, my colleague and myself inclined to the view that the effect of marginality was not a consequence of electors' calculating that it was more vital to vote in more marginal seats, but was a result of the fact that the parties' campaign efforts are greater in these seats. In our second report, however, we argued that things had changed in the 1970s, and that the stronger correlations between marginality and turnout reflected the fact that 'voters respond less to the stimulus of the party campaigns, and more to their own independent assessments of the likelihood of seats changing hands' (p. 387).

Even when the effects of social variables like owner-occupation and political variables like marginality are added together, however, there still remains a good deal of turnout variation that is unexplained. On the one hand, seats in Wales and in parts of Scotland have higher turnouts than would be expected. This seems to be a product of local traditions or cultural norms. Similarly, seats in coal-mining areas have unusually high turnouts (although this has not been as marked in recent elections), and this too reflects the traditions of such areas, as well as the role of community cohesion referred to above. On the other hand, lower than expected turnouts are found in English conurbations, especially inner-city areas. To some extent, this may be a result of more inaccurate electoral registers but it also reflects the fact that these areas have large transient and unstable populations, as well as higher levels of poverty and deprivation.

Studying voting as opposed to non-voting by means of surveys is not easy. Survey respondents tend to claim that they voted when they actually did not and, as a result, there are often relatively few cases of non-voters to analyse. To date, the most substantial consideration of the topic at individual level is by Crewe, Fox and Alt (1977), who use BES survey data from the four general elections between 1966 and October 1974. They find, first of all, that very few people are consistent non-voters. If someone fails to vote in one election, he or she is quite likely to vote in the one after or the one after that. This is linked to the reasons for failing to vote, which are overwhelmingly 'accidental' or 'apathetic'. People may be away on polling day, or ill, or simply forget to vote. Very few are deliberate abstainers in the sense of refusing to vote on principle.

Crewe et al. investigate the effects of a series of social variables on propensity to vote and find that most seem to have little effect. Working-class people are as likely to vote as middle-class, women as likely as men, the poorly educated as likely as the highly educated, and so on. Only four factors seem to be associated with poor turnout: being young, being single, living in privately rented accommodation and being residentially mobile. These are clearly strongly interconnected and they all involve isolation from social pressure, characteristic of stable communities, to conform to the norm of voting. The archetypal non-voter is a single young person who has recently moved into a bed-sit in South Kensington. These survey findings fit well with the interpretations of aggregate analyses which, as we have seen, also emphasise the role of stable as opposed to transient communities in explaining turnout variations.

The most important political variable affecting the individual voter's propensity to turn out in elections is strength of party identification. This is consistently found in studies of electoral participation. Butler and Stokes (1974, p. 40) found in the early 1960s that 64 per cent of very strong identifiers voted in local elections compared with 54 per cent of fairly strong identifiers and 39 per cent of not very strong identifiers. Figures from the analysis by Crewe and his colleagues are given in Table 6.5, and the pattern is very clear.

The importance of party identification strength suggests an interpretation of the trend in overall aggregate turnout which was reported in Table 6.2. Turnout, it might be argued, was higher in the 1950s and 1960s because there were more strong identifiers in the electorate then. As the strength of party identification decreased thereafter, turnout settled at a lower level. This is, of course, far from a full explanation of the trend in turnout, and the decline in party identification offers few clues about how to account for cross-sectional variation. But the generally lower level of national turnout in the 1970s and 1980s may be a consequence of partisan dealignment that is easily overlooked.

Table 6.5 Regularity of voting by strength of party identification (%)

	Very strong	Fairly strong	Not very strong
Regular voters	84	74	54

Source: Crewe, Fox and Alt (1977).
Note: The figures are the percentages who voted in all four general
elections from 1966 to October 1974.

Patterns of party support, 1950–70

In Chapter 2, I described the period 1950 to 1970 as, electorally, a period of alignment. Surveys revealed that voters were mainly influenced by long-term factors. They were aligned with the Conservative or Labour party and their vote was stable from election to election. To what extent is this mirrored in election results?

The distribution of votes at each election between 1950 and 1970 is given in Table 6.6 and the figures demonstrate, firstly, the electoral dominance of the two major parties. Their combined share of the votes averaged 91.8 per cent in these elections. (In terms of seats two-party dominance was even greater, with an average of 98.5 per cent of seats won by the two parties). Not surprisingly, the two parties monopolised government, with Labour holding office from 1950 to 1951 and 1964 to 1970, and the Conservatives being in power from 1951 to 1964.

Secondly, the relative stability of support for the two major parties is also impressive. Over the 20 years, neither reached 50 per cent of the votes cast and neither fell below 40 per cent. Liberal support was rather more variable but this was largely due to variations in the number of Liberal candidates. The sharp rise in the votes obtained by 'others' in 1970 reflects the increased support obtained by the nationalist parties in Scotland and Wales at that election.

There was, of course, some change in support for the major parties from election to election. As measured by overall swing,[2] however, such changes tended to be small, with the exception of 1970 which was in many ways a watershed election. As I noted in Chapter 1, swing is a measure of net change in elections and it is likely that there was more individual change than the gross figures imply. None the less, the election results from 1950 to 1970 are very much what would be expected on

Table 6.6   National distribution of votes, 1950–70 (%)

	1950	1951	1955	1959	1964	1966	1970
Conservative	43.5	48.0	49.7	49.4	43.4	41.9	46.4
Labour	46.1	48.8	46.4	43.8	44.1	47.9	43.0
Liberal	9.1	2.5	2.7	5.9	11.2	8.5	7.5
Others	1.3	0.7	1.1	1.0	1.3	1.6	3.1
Overall swing	—	+0.9	+2.9	+1.2	−3.2	−2.7	+4.7

Source: Butler and Kavanagh (1988, p. 283).

the basis of the model of individual voting outlined in Chapter 2. Partisan and class alignment among voters sustained a stable two-party system at aggregate level.

One further feature of general election results in this period should be noted. Changes in the distribution of votes from one election to the next were remarkably uniform over the country as a whole. As Crewe puts it:

> In every election but one (1959) at least three-quarters of the constituency swings were within 2 per cent of the national median and only a handful of seats bucked the national trend. To know the swing in Cornwall was to know, within a percentage point or two, the swing in the Highlands; to know the results of the first three constituencies to declare on election night was to know not only which party had won — but by how many seats (1985, pp. 101–3).

The last point is something of an exaggeration but it is a pardonable one. Significant deviations from the national trend were relatively rare.

Exactly why swing in British elections was so uniform in this period is something of a mystery. A commonsense explanation might suggest that uniform swing was produced by uniform behaviour. Over the country as a whole, we might think, voters responded in the same way to national issues and events which are transmitted by national media during a national election campaign. But in this case common sense would be wrong. If, say, 5 per cent of Labour voters in one election switched to the Conservatives at the next, in every constituency, this would not produce uniform swing. The reason is that 5 per cent of Labour voters in a safe Labour seat represents many more people than 5 per cent of Labour voters in a safe Conservative seat. In a safe Labour seat, therefore, a switch of this kind would have a far greater effect on the share of votes obtained by the parties than in a safe Conservative seat with only a small number of Labour voters in the first place. Consequently, the swing figures would be different.[3]

Butler and Stokes (1974, pp. 140–51) directly addressed the problem of uniform swing and suggested that it could be explained by the fact that, in any individual constituency, voters are influenced by both national and local forces. They argued that the influence of the local environment dampened or accentuated national movements and that these forces balanced out in such a way that swing tended to be uniform. It remains very difficult to explain, however, why uniformity of swing should result from these processes.

Although uniform swing between pairs of elections was the rule between 1950 and 1970, there were two distinct cumulative trends in swing which began in the 1959 election. In the first place, in every election from 1959 to 1970 there was a tendency for constituencies in more urban areas to swing more heavily than average to Labour, when the national trend was in Labour's favour, and less heavily than average to the Conservatives (or even in the opposite direction) when the national swing was in *their* favour. In more rural seats the opposite was the case. Secondly, there were similar cumulative movements towards Labour in Scotland and the North of England, and towards the Conservatives in the South of England and the Midlands.

Both of these trends are illustrated in Table 6.7, which shows deviations from the total swing between 1955 and 1970 in constituencies grouped according to region and degree of urbanisation. The pattern is remarkably regular. There are clear differences between the regions but within each region there is also a divergence between urban and rural areas. These trends continued after 1970 and had important consequences for the operation of the electoral system which I consider below.

Until the late 1960s the analysis of aggregate election statistics was normally confined to the election results themselves (as in the statistical appendices to the Nuffield studies). There were very few examples of analysis that attempted to relate the distribution of party support in constituencies to their socio-economic characteristics in a systematic way.

Table 6.7   Deviations in swing, 1955−70

	South of England/ Midlands	North of England	Scotland	All
City	−1.0	−6.5	−8.5	−3.9
Very urban	+1.1	−4.6	−8.0	−2.8
Mainly urban	+2.2	−1.1	−5.8	−0.1
Mixed	+4.0	+0.8	−4.8	+1.4
Mainly rural	+4.6	−0.4	−1.1	+3.2
Very rural	+6.0	+2.3	−0.4	+2.7
All	+2.2	−2.0	−4.8	

Source: Curtice and Steed (1986, p. 212).

Notes: Each entry is the difference between the mean two-party swing in the category of constituency concerned and the mean for all constituencies. A plus sign indicates a deviation in favour of the Conservatives and a minus sign a deviation in favour of Labour. Wales is excluded from the table.

The reason for this was that it was not until the sample census of 1966 that census data were made available on a constituency basis.

In the Nuffield study of the 1970 election, however, Ivor Crewe and Clive Payne (1971) demonstrated the possibilities for aggregate analysis that had been opened up by the availability of census data for constituencies. Among other things, they calculated the correlations between a variety of socio-economic factors and party shares of the vote, and a selection of these is reproduced in Table 6.8.

The occupational class composition of constituencies (% non-manual) produced the best single correlation with party support, although the class-related housing variables (% owner-occupiers, % council tenants) also correlated well. The very small figures for % young voters and % born in the New Commonwealth are useful reminders of the pitfalls of inferring individual behaviour from aggregate statistics. We know from survey data that, as a matter of fact, both of these groups disproportionately supported Labour. In most constituencies, however, they constituted such a small fraction of the electorate that variations in their size had no impact on the votes received by the parties, and hence the correlations are weak.

A more exhaustive analysis of the social correlates of constituency voting patterns in the 1966 general election was undertaken by Miller (1977). I shall return to this analysis below, but for the moment it should be noted that Miller examined the effect of 42 socio-economic variables upon levels of party support and found that 'when the census variables were used to predict Labour versus Conservative votes in the constituencies, the occupation variables were by far the most effective' (p. 27). Easily the most important single measure was the percentage of employers and managers in a constituency, which had a correlation of 0.71 with % Conservative and −0.84 with % Labour. The class character of a constituency was, then, the best guide to its political character.

Table 6.8 Correlations between socio-economic characteristics of English constituencies and party shares of votes, 1970

	% Con.	% Lab.		% Con.	% Lab.
% non-manual	0.59	−0.60	% young voters	0.03	0.02
% manual	−0.31	0.38	% aged 65+	0.42	−0.49
% owner-occupiers	0.53	−0.55	% female	0.30	−0.29
% council tenants	−0.37	0.42	% born in New Commonwealth	−0.06	0.12

Source: Crewe and Payne (1971, p. 419).

In general terms, the results of these sorts of analysis were not exactly news to any observer of British electoral politics. Most people knew that middle-class areas usually returned Conservative MPs and that working-class areas voted Labour. However, aggregate-data analysis, at the least, brought a new precision to knowledge of this kind. Correlation coefficients enabled researchers to tell exactly how strongly certain characteristics of constituencies were related to levels of party support, and regression equations clarified the nature of such relationships. The availability of appropriate data allowed more subtle and sophisticated analysis of election results than had hitherto been possible.

Examination of aggregate voting patterns from 1950 to 1970, then, seems to fulfil the expectations that we would have on the basis of the discussion of individual voting behaviour in Chapter 2. The two major parties dominated elections, their support was stable, inter-election change was relatively small and variations in constituency voting patterns were best explained by variations in class composition. I have suggested in earlier chapters, however, that there were major changes in voting behaviour after 1970 and we must now consider the extent to which these are reflected in aggregate patterns.

Patterns of party support, 1970–87

After 1970 survey studies argued that voters were increasingly dealigned. They were not as strongly committed to the major parties as before and the connections between class and party support became weaker. Voters were more volatile and more influenced by short-term electoral forces.

Given this, we might expect that election results would show more volatility. With the stabilising influence of class and party identification reduced, change rather than stability is to be expected. It is not, however, quite as straightforward as this. It is possible, for instance, that short-term forces could favour the same party in successive elections, or that increased volatility at the individual level could be self-cancelling. In these cases the election results would give the appearance of stability. The absence of sharp swings in elections cannot in itself, then, be taken as a refutation of the dealignment thesis. On the other hand, sharp net changes in at least some elections would constitute strong evidence of a more dealigned electorate.

The shares of votes received by the parties in general elections from 1970 to 1987 are shown in Table 6.9. Clearly, the two major parties

Table 6.9 National distribution of votes, 1970−87 (%)

	1970	Feb. 1974	Oct. 1974	1979	1983	1987
Conservative	46.4	37.8	35.8	43.9	42.4	42.3
Labour	43.0	37.1	39.2	37.0	27.6	30.8
Liberal/Alliance	7.5	19.3	18.3	13.8	25.4	22.6
Others	3.1	5.8	6.7	5.3	4.6	4.3
Overall swing	—	−1.4	−2.1	+5.2	+4.0	−1.7

Source: Butler and Kavanagh (1988, p. 283).

experienced a sharp decline in popularity during this period. Their combined support had averaged 91.8 per cent of the vote in the seven elections to 1970 but averaged only 74.8 per cent in the five elections after that. Neither the Conservatives nor Labour reached the level of support they had averaged between 1950 and 1970 in a single election thereafter. This electoral decline was not reflected in the House of Commons where the two parties continued to dominate, with only a slightly reduced average of 94.0 per cent of seats won. Even this slight reduction made it more difficult for one party to gain an overall majority of seats: in the second half of the 1970s the Labour government lost its majority and had to rely on the support of Liberals and others to stay in office.

Support for the two parties was also more variable than before. The Conservative share of votes fell by more than 10 points between 1970 and October 1974 before recovering to stabilise under Mrs Thatcher from 1979 onwards. In the 1983 election, on the other hand, Labour recorded its lowest vote share since 1918 and was more than 15 points below its 1970 level.

The other side of the coin to reduced major-party support is, of course, increased support for the Liberals and, from 1983, the Alliance. The Liberals by themselves achieved a remarkable leap of almost 12 points between 1970 and February 1974 but fell away somewhat after that. In 1981, however, a new party — the SDP — was formed as a breakaway from Labour. The fact that a new party could be formed and immediately attract high levels of public support is itself an indicator of the fluid nature of party loyalties at this time. The SDP and the Liberals fought the 1983 and 1987 elections together as the Alliance, and their share of the vote in 1983 was the highest 'third-party' vote since 1923.

The higher level of support for 'others' after 1970, which the table shows, is in part simply a reflection of a change in the way in which votes cast in Northern Ireland are now categorised.[4] But it also reflects more nationalist voting in Scotland and Wales.

Despite the increased variability in major-party support after 1970, the figures for swing shown in Table 6.9 are not very remarkable. It is true that the 5.2 per cent swing recorded in 1979 was the largest since the war and the 1983 swing was also higher than the post-war average. But the other three swings were relatively small. This might appear to contradict the claim that variability in levels of party support increased during this period. But swing is a measure of the relative changes in support for the two major parties only: it does not directly take account of the performances of other parties.

A measure of net electoral change which does do this is the Pedersen index (named after its inventor, Mogens Pedersen, a Danish political scientist). This index is created by adding together the percentage-point change in *all* parties' shares of the vote between two elections and dividing the result by two. Thus, from Table 6.9 the changes between 1983 and 1987 were 0.1 (Conservative), 3.2 (Labour), 2.8 (Alliance) and 0.3 (others). These sum to 6.4, so the index score is 3.2.

Table 6.10 shows the index score for post-war elections. Overall, the scores after 1970 average 8.1 compared with 4.9 for 1970 and before. Two post-1970 elections have low scores (October 1974, which followed very shortly after the previous election, and 1987). As I explained above, however, these indications of low aggregate volatility do not, in themselves, contradict the argument that individual voting was more dealigned. On the other hand, the very high scores in the three other post-1970 elections are clear reflections at aggregate level of dealignment at the level of the individual voter.

Changes in party support in individual constituencies after 1970 have been characterised by an increase in variability. The days of a nationally

Table 6.10 Pedersen index scores, 1951–87

1951	7.7	Feb. 1974	14.5
1955	2.4	Oct. 1974	3.0
1959	3.1	1979	8.1
1964	6.0	1983	11.6
1966	4.2	1987	3.2
1970	6.0		

uniform swing have gone. As I mentioned in Chapter 1, the spread or dispersion of a set of scores is measured by the standard deviation. The standard deviations of constituency swings in elections since 1959 are shown in Table 6.11.

The standard deviations were fairly constant until 1979 but since then have been larger, indicating greater variability in swing from constituency to constituency. The distance we have travelled, as it were, from uniform swing is well illustrated by McAllister and Rose (1984, p. 199), who note that the pattern of change between 1979 and 1983 implied by the national swing (a rise in the Conservative vote and a decline in the Labour vote) occurred in only 71 of the seats in which these two parties finished in first and second places. In 209 such seats both of them lost support. Where the Conservative and the Alliance were the front runners, both increased their vote in 129 constituencies, while in 159 seats the Alliance vote increased and that of the Conservatives declined.

It is not easy to convey the meaning and the extent of the increased variability of swing in figures. The standard deviation is not an easy statistic to interpret. However, a visual impression of what the increasing standard deviation of swing means is given in Figure 6.1, which shows the approximate distribution of constituencies around the mean swing in 1966 and 1987. In 1966 most constituencies were closely bunched around the mean. The graph for 1987 is much flatter and more spread out. It is this difference that the relevant standard deviation statistics indicate.

The increased variation in constituency swings has been partly caused by the continuation and acceleration of the deviating trends which began in 1959. In every election until 1987, whatever its direction on national figures, swing deviated towards Labour in the North of England, Scotland and more urban seats, whereas in the Midlands, the South and more rural areas it deviated towards the Conservatives. The cumulative effects of

Table 6.11 Standard deviation of two-party swings, 1959—87

1959	1964	1966	1970	Oct. 1974	1979	1983	1987
2.7	3.1	2.1	2.6	2.4	4.1	5.1	4.1

Sources: Curtice and Steed (1980, p. 394; 1984, p. 334; 1988, p. 317).
Note: The election of February 1974 is omitted because constituency boundary changes make the computation of swings problematical.

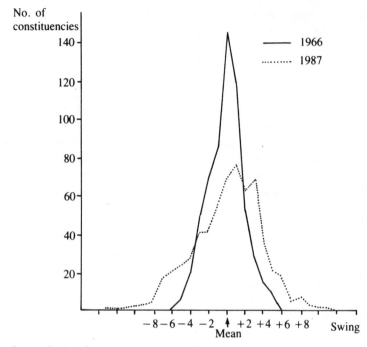

Source: Derived from diagrams in Steed (1966) and Curtice and Steed (1988).

Figure 6.1   Distribution of two-party swing across constituencies, 1966 and 1987

these movements between 1970 and 1979 are illustrated in Table 6.12, which is of the same form as Table 6.7. As in the 1955–70 period the pattern here is remarkably regular, with both regional and urban/rural deviations from the national trend being very marked.

Taking Tables 6.7 and 6.12 together, the long-term cumulative divergences in swing are enormous. At the extremes, between 1955 and 1979 the swing in very rural constituencies in the Midlands and South of England deviated from the national figure by a total of 12.3 points towards the Conservatives, while cities in Scotland deviated by 19.1 points towards Labour. Over the country as a whole, there was a swing of 1.8 per cent towards the Conservatives between 1955 and 1979, but rural areas in the South and Midlands had a 14.1 per cent swing to the Conservatives and Scottish cities swung 17.3 per cent to Labour.

Curtice and Steed do not give exactly comparable figures for the 1983 election but the pattern of the previous elections was repeated, with

Table 6.12 Deviations in swing, 1970–79

	South of England/ Midlands	North of England	Scotland	All
City	−2.2	−7.2	−10.6	−4.5
Very urban	−1.0	−4.3	−9.6	−2.8
Mainly urban	+1.8	−3.1	−6.7	−0.8
Mixed	+3.8	+0.3	−2.7	+2.0
Mainly rural	+5.4	+1.3	−2.2	+3.8
Very rural	+6.3	+5.3	+1.5	+6.0
All	+1.8	−2.4	−5.3	

Source: Curtice and Steed (1980, p. 212).
Note: As Table 6.7.

swings ranging from 11.0 per cent to the Conservatives in the rural Midlands to 2.5 per cent to Labour in urban Scotland (Curtice and Steed 1984, p. 338). In the 1987 election, regional deviations appeared yet again (the extremes being 2.3 per cent to the Conservatives in the South of England and 5.3 per cent to Labour in Scotland) but there was no marked urban/rural divergence.

A final summary of regional trends in swing is given in Table 6.13. This shows the mean regional deviations from the national swing from 1955 to 1970, from 1970 to 1987, and for the whole period. In each case, except for Wales, divergences after 1970 are in the same direction as in the earlier period and are noticeably sharper in three of the four other regions. By the 1980s talk of an electoral 'North–South divide' was common. Like most generalisations, the idea of an electoral

Table 6.13 Long-term regional deviations in two-party swing

	1955–70	1970–87	Total 1955–87
South of England	+1.7	+7.2	+8.9
Midlands	+3.1	+2.8	+5.9
North of England	−2.0	−7.0	−9.0
Scotland	−4.8	−14.3	−19.1
Wales	−1.9	+3.5	+0.6

Source: Curtice and Steed (1988, p. 330).
Note: As Table 6.7.

dichotomy between the North and South of the country is an over-simplification, but it does highlight a major feature of the current pattern of party support in Britain.[5]

In Chapter 2, I briefly noted some explanations for regional divergence in elections up to 1970. The accentuation of regional differences after 1970 has focused more attention on the problem. Curtice and Steed (1982) suggest that there are three main explanations for the trend. Firstly, there have been slow changes in the distribution of socio-economic characteristics among the electorate. The proportion of broadly middle-class people has tended to increase in the South and in rural areas and, relatively speaking, to decrease in the North, Scotland and urban areas. Secondly, differential regional behaviour, even within classes, is a product of regional variations in economic well-being. Put crudely, Scotland and the North are simply not as prosperous as the South. Thirdly, there is a purely political factor. As third parties have increased in popularity, this has generally been at the expense of the locally weaker major party. Since the Conservatives were already weaker in the North and Scotland, they suffered more from the increase in support for the Liberals, Alliance and SNP after 1970. They thus performed poorly relative to Labour and this is reflected in the swing figures. In the South, the picture is reversed with Labour being the party to suffer.

Some of these arguments are expanded upon by Johnston et al. (1988) in a thorough analysis of regional variations in recent elections. They argue that recent government policy has had a differential regional impact, including changes in levels of unemployment, the occupational and industrial structure and property values. Opinion poll data show that these have resulted in regional variations in satisfaction with the country's economic performance and in optimism about the economic future. In turn, this is reflected in divergences in regional voting patterns.

These sorts of consideration are mainly directed to explaining changes in regional patterns of party support since 1955 (or even more recently), and they certainly shed a good deal of light on them. It is, however, still difficult to account for the very long-standing regional differences which have been clear since at least 1918. At root, as Curtice and Steed imply, these are likely to be a product of 'cultural or historical differences and defy economic interpretations' (1988, p. 333).

The long-term divergences in party support — both regionally and as between urban and rural areas — have had important consequences for the operation of the British electoral system. These are explored in detail by Curtice and Steed (1986). Formerly, the share of seats that a party would obtain in the House of Commons, on the basis of a given share of the total national vote, could be predicted fairly well by using the 'cube law'. If the share of votes between two parties were in the ratio A:B, then the share of seats would be in the ratio $A^3:B^3$. Thus, if the ratio of the two-party vote were 3:2, the ratio of seats would be 27.8 ($3 \times 3 \times 3 : 2 \times 2 \times 2$). In other words, the party which obtained 60 per cent of the votes would get 77 per cent of the seats, while the other party with 40 per cent of the votes would get only 23 per cent of the seats. Clearly, then, the winning party's lead in terms of votes was greatly exaggerated by the electoral system when it was translated into seats.

The trends in support since 1955, however, have had the effect of making Labour seats more safely Labour and Conservative seats more safely Conservative. As a result, there have been fewer and fewer marginal seats. In 1955, 166 seats could be classed as marginal but by 1983 there were only 80 (Curtice and Steed 1986, p. 214). There are now fewer seats for a party to gain for each percentage point swing in its favour, and fewer will be lost by incumbents for each point of swing against their party. Much bigger swings in votes are now required for the party in opposition to gain enough seats to achieve a majority in the House of Commons. The exaggerative quality of the electoral system has declined such that the ratio of seats to votes can no longer be predicted by a 'cube law' or even a 'square law'.

The publication of census data for parliamentary constituencies, which began in 1966, was continued for the censuses of 1971 and 1981. This has given rise to a flourishing industry in the aggregate analysis of election data. It is impossible to summarise this extensive literature here so I will confine discussion to two important points.

The first centres on the data reproduced in Table 6.14, which show the correlations between seven socio-economic variables and the shares of votes received by the three leading parties in British constituencies in the 1987 general election. What these coefficients indicate is that there is still a very strong relationship between the socio-economic characteristics of a constituency and the level of its support for the Labour and Conservative parties. Indeed, the correlations here are stronger than the comparable figures given in Table 6.8 for the 1970 election. The correlations between Alliance support and these social characteristics, however, are only moderate. This is something that is generally true of support for third parties in Britain — it is always less strongly related to the socio-economic characteristics of constituencies than is support for Labour or the Conservatives. Put another way, the level of third-party support in a constituency is less predictable than support for the other parties. This applies to the SNP as well as to the Liberals and the Alliance, and it is likely to apply in future to the Democrats. It is probably a function of the fact that these parties do not attempt to appeal directly to specific social groups. The relatively weak aggregate correlations for Alliance support — although they indicate some structuring by socio-economic characteristics — tend to confirm survey findings that Alliance support is more evenly spread across social groups than is support for the major parties.

The second discussion point also arises directly out of the data in Table 6.14. I have argued that at the individual level voting behaviour in Britain after 1970 was characterised by a loosening of the relationship between social characteristics — especially social class — and party choice. Yet the table shows very strong correlations at aggregate level between the class make-up of constituencies (% employers and managers and % working class) and the level of support for the Conservatives and Labour. Indeed, these correlations are stronger for the 1987 election than they were in 1966 or 1970. This appears to contradict the thesis of class dealignment.

In fact, the discrepancy between aggregate and individual data is more apparent than real. The fact that % employers and managers correlates strongly with % Conservative means that the bigger the proportion of

Table 6.14 Correlations between socio-economic characteristics of constituencies and party shares of vote, 1987

	% Conservative	% Labour	% Alliance
% unemployed	−0.73	0.75	−0.42
% employers and managers	0.78	−0.83	0.48
% working class	−0.77	0.82	−0.48
% with degree	0.41	−0.50	0.31
% car owners	0.74	−0.78	0.45
% owner-occupiers	0.68	−0.60	0.31
% council tenants	−0.72	0.68	−0.38

Source: Butler and Kavanagh (1988, p. 286).

employers and managers in a constituency the higher is the Conservative share of the vote. However, this might reflect the fact that the more employers and managers there are, the more everyone, irrespective of their class, votes Conservative. It tells us nothing about the extent of individual class voting.

In his work on this problem, however, Miller (1977, 1978, 1979) has shown that the relationship between the class character of constituencies and their vote is stronger than would be expected on the basis of any given level of individual class voting. Where the Conservatives would be expected to do well on the basis of the class composition of the constituency, they do even better; where they would be expected to do badly they do even worse. The same applies to Labour. Constituencies, in short, are more polarised politically than people. The correlations at aggregate level are stronger, therefore, than the correlation at individual level.

Once again this is perfectly compatible with individual dealignment. Indeed, if more and more working-class people vote Conservative in predominantly middle-class areas, and more and more middle-class people vote Labour in predominantly working-class areas, the effect would be to produce both increased polarisation at the constituency level and decreased class voting at the level of the individual voter.

The question remains, however, as to why the constituency effect occurs: why do people tend to follow locally dominant political norms irrespective of class? Miller's answer is a version of the 'neighbourhood' effect discussed briefly in Chapter 2. The crucial feature of a voter's local environment is the concentration (or absence) of what Miller sees as 'core' classes. These are the 'controllers' (employers and managers) and 'anti-controllers' (manual workers who are trade union members). Concentrations of these classes set the tone, as it were, of an area and their influence is reinforced by personal contacts. As Miller put it, 'Those who speak together vote together' (1977, p. 65). He concludes that:

> the class characteristics of the social environment have more effect on constituency partisanship than class differences themselves . . . the partisanship of individuals is influenced more by where they live than what they do.

There is no conflict, then, between the aggregate data statistics shown in Table 6.14 and the general interpretation of trends in voting behaviour which I have advanced in previous chapters. The spatial polarisation of support for the two major parties has itself contributed to a damping down of the effect of traditional social cleavages.

Conclusion

Before 1970, general election results were marked by two-party dominance and by stability. Aligned voting among individuals sustained a cohesive, class-based, stable two-party system. After 1970, dealignment increased and the party system became more fragmented. Elections were marked by instability and fluidity. In the final chapter I will look in more detail at the 1987 election, and speculate a little about how British electoral politics might develop in the next few years.

Notes

1. This has been the number of constituencies in the United Kingdom since 1983. In most analyses, the 17 constituencies in Northern Ireland are omitted. The total number of constituencies has been slowly increasing in the post-war period. In the elections of 1950 and 1951 there were 625, from 1955 to 1970 there were 630, and from February 1974 to 1979 there were 635.
2. 'Overall' swing is calculated from the distribution of votes over the country as a whole. It should be distinguished from *mean* swing, which is the average of swings in all the individual constituencies.
3. For further explanation and discussion of this somewhat difficult point, see McLean (1973).
4. Until 1970 Ulster Unionist MPs took the Conservative party whip in the House of Commons, and Unionist votes were routinely added to the Conservative total. After 1970, however, the Unionist monolith fragmented (as did the traditional nationalist vote in the province) and Unionist MPs distanced themselves from the Conservatives. Since February 1974 the convention has been to treat all votes cast in Northern Ireland as 'others'.
5. The regional distribution of votes in the 1987 election is given in Table 7.2.

7

The 1987 General Election and the Electoral Outlook

The 1987 election

The result of the 1987 general election was a surprise to most observers. It was not the fact of the Conservative victory that was surprising but its scale. Between 1983 and 1987 the Conservative record in local elections and by-elections had been dismal and their opinion poll rating mediocre. The chances of the general election producing a 'hung' Parliament — a situation in which no one party has a majority over all the others combined — appeared good. Even on election night itself, computer projections based on last-minute and exit polls markedly underestimated the size of the Conservative majority in the House of Commons.

In the event (see Table 7.1), the Conservatives almost repeated their smashing victory of 1983. Their share of the vote was almost identical while Labour made a modest recovery and the Alliance slipped back a bit. The Tories won an overall majority of 102 seats.

Perhaps the most striking feature of the 1987 results was the absence of uniform movement across the country. A simple indicator of this is that, very unusually, the three major parties and the SNP all gained some seats and lost others. It was, indeed, the absence of uniform change that largely explains why computer projections of the distribution of seats on the basis of polls went awry, although the polls themselves predicted the distribution of votes with considerable accuracy.

Table 7.1 General election result, 1987

	Share of votes (%)	Change 1983–87	Seats	Change 1983–87
Conservative	42.3	−0.1	376	−21
Labour	30.8	+3.2	229	+20
Alliance	22.6	−2.8	22	−1
Others	4.3	−0.3	23	+2

Source: Butler and Kavanagh (1988, p. 283).

Table 7.2 Regional variations in party support, 1987

	Distribution of votes			Change in share 1983–87		
	Con. (%)	Lab. (%)	All. (%)	Con.	Lab.	All.
Scotland	24.0	42.4	19.2	−4.3	+7.3	−5.3
Wales	29.5	45.1	17.9	−1.5	+7.5	−5.3
England	46.2	29.5	23.8	+0.2	+2.6	−2.6
North	32.3	46.4	21.0	−2.3	+6.2	−4.0
Yorks/Humberside	37.4	40.6	21.7	−1.2	+5.3	−3.9
North West	38.0	41.2	20.6	−2.0	+5.2	−3.0
West Midlands	45.5	33.3	20.8	+0.5	+2.1	−2.6
East Midlands	48.6	30.0	21.0	+1.4	+2.1	−3.1
East Anglia	52.1	21.7	25.7	+1.1	+1.2	−2.5
South East	52.2	22.3	25.0	+1.7	+1.1	−2.4
South West	50.6	15.9	33.0	−0.8	+1.2	−0.2

Source: Butler and Kavanagh (1988, p. 284).
Notes: In Scotland the SNP obtained 14.0% of the vote (+2.3 as compared with 1983).
In Wales Plaid Cymru obtained 7.3%, a decline of 0.5. Percentages do not total
100 because votes for 'others' are not shown.

The most striking variations in the results were regional. Table 7.2
shows the 1987 distribution of votes, together with changes in vote shares
since 1983, separately for Scotland, Wales, England and the English
regions. The Conservatives increased their support in England but drop-
ped back in Wales and, more sharply, in Scotland; Labour's advance
was more pronounced in Scotland and Wales, and here too the Alliance
declined more than elsewhere. Within England, however, there were

clear regional variations. The 'two nations' of the prosperous South and the depressed North diverged still further politically. The more northern regions moved more heavily away from the Conservatives and towards Labour than did the others. In the South East of the country, indeed, there was a net swing to the Conservatives. The pattern is broken, however, in the South West where the Conservatives performed relatively poorly and the Alliance relatively well.

The figures for the distribution of votes show clearly the extent to which support for the two major parties is now geographically concentrated. The Conservatives have more than 45 per cent of the vote in every region from the Midlands southwards but less than 30 per cent in Wales and Scotland. Labour has more than 40 per cent in the three most northerly English regions and in Wales and Scotland, but is very weak everywhere else. In contrast, the Alliance vote is spread relatively evenly, with only Wales and the South West deviating markedly from the overall average. The effect of these patterns of voting support for the parties is that party representation in the House of Commons is geographically skewed. After the 1987 election, only 81 of the 376 Conservative MPs represented constituencies in Scotland, Wales or the North of England. On the other hand, 170 of the 229 Labour MPs came from these areas and only 59 came from the whole of the rest of England.

One source of constituency variation which did not appear in the 1987 election to the extent expected was tactical voting. In by-elections between 1983 and 1987 there had been very clear evidence of tactical voting (see Denver 1988), and in the run-up to the general election the idea was widely discussed in the media. There certainly was *some* tactical voting in the election — especially involving the SNP in some Scottish seats — with third-placed parties being 'squeezed'. But it did not occur on anything like the scale that would have been necessary to affect the outcome of the election significantly.

At the time of writing, the BES report on the 1987 election has yet to be published. Opinion poll results became available almost immediately after the election, however, and I have reported some of these in previous chapters. Here, Table 7.3 shows how different groups in the electorate voted.

Confirming recent trends, there was hardly any difference between men and women in respect of party choice. In terms of age, Labour did best among the youngest voters but, even so, did not regain their traditional advantage among the young. Conservative support increased with age (a familiar pattern) whereas Alliance support decreased somewhat.

Table 7.3 Party choice of selected social groups, 1987 (%)

	Conservative	Labour	Alliance
All	43	32	23
Men	41	33	23
Women	43	31	23
Aged 18−29	36	35	26
30−44	41	31	26
45−64	44	31	22
65+	47	31	21
Homeowners	47	25	25
Council tenants	22	58	14
Professional/managerial	54	13	30
Clerical	47	24	26
Skilled manual	42	35	21
Other manual	31	46	20

Source: ITN/Harris exit poll reported in *Independent*, 13/6/87.
Note: Percentages should be read across rows. The figures do not total 100 because votes
     for other parties are excluded.

Older people appear to be more set in their ways and relatively disinclined
to vote for a new party. The differences between homeowners and council
tenants are marked, with a clear majority of the latter voting Labour
as compared with only 1 in 4 of the former.

Occupational class clearly still affects voting choice. The Conservative
share of votes is larger and Labour's smaller among the non-manual
groups. None the less, the evidence in the table suggests that the decline
in class voting is continuing. Only one group (professional and managerial
workers) gave a majority of its votes to one party, and for the second
successive election a plurality of skilled manual workers voted Conservative. Moreover, when compared with equivalent 1983 data, the figures
for occupation and vote indicate a swing to Labour among non-manual
workers and a swing to the Conservatives among manual workers.[1] Full
discussion of the question of the trend in class voting must, however,
await the publication of the BES report.

One further feature of the occupation data is worthy of note — the
relative evenness of Alliance support across classes. Although the
Alliance did somewhat better among non-manual than among manual
groups, its vote is much less skewed by class than are the votes of the

other parties. Crewe (1987a) reports, however, that the Alliance did have a special appeal to one segment of the population — those who have had a university education. Among this (very small) group the Alliance was the most popular party, with 36 per cent of the three-party vote.

In Chapter 3, I mentioned the distinction which Ivor Crewe makes between the 'traditional' and a 'new' working class. A large part of Labour's lack of electoral success in recent years can be attributed to its failure to attract adequate support among the latter group. The party choice of manual workers in 1987, differentiated according to region, housing tenure, union membership and sector of employment, is shown in Table 7.4.

Labour polled quite satisfactorily among the traditional working class, although it is worth noting that the party failed to obtain a majority of the votes of union members or public-sector workers. Among workers who live in the South or are owner-occupiers, however, Labour trailed badly and their support among workers who are not members of unions or who work in the private sector was not very substantial. A major problem for Labour is that the 'new' working class is larger than the old and is increasing in size, while the traditional working class is becoming smaller.

Table 7.4 Party choice of manual workers, 1987 (%)

| | 'New' working class | | | |
	Lives in South	Owner-occupier	Non-union	Private sector
Conservative	46	44	40	38
Labour	28	32	38	39
Alliance	26	24	22	23
	'Traditional' working class			
	Lives in Scotland/ North	Council tenant	Union member	Public sector
Conservative	29	25	30	32
Labour	57	57	48	49
Alliance	15	18	22	19

Source: Crewe (1987a).

The electoral outlook

Predicting future electoral trends — unlike 'predicting' from regression equations — is a hazardous business. It is particularly hazardous in Britain today because of the change from aligned to dealigned voting, which I have emphasised throughout this book. A commentator on elections writing in, say, 1955 could have felt confident in assuming that in the next few elections the two major parties would continue to dominate and that in terms of popular support they would not be very far apart. The electoral turmoil of the 1970s was still some way distant. With a dealigned, more free-floating electorate, however, the electoral situation is altogether more complex. None the less, I will conclude this review of electoral behaviour in Britain by considering briefly how the developments which have been discussed have affected the major parties, and by speculating a little about what the future might hold for them.

The Conservatives

Following the 1987 election the Conservative party appears to be sitting pretty. They have won their third successive election and in each of them their share of the vote has been very stable. Long-term social changes — the contraction of the traditional working class, the increase in home ownership, the movement of population from the North to the South — have worked to their advantage and will continue to do so. In other words, social groups which have favoured the Conservatives are increasing in size. In addition, in the last two elections the opposition to the Conservatives has been divided. The split in the Labour party which led to the formation of the SDP meant that Labour's position as the sole credible alternative to the Conservatives was seriously undermined. Anti-Conservative voters were no longer concentrated in one party. In Scotland and Wales non-Conservatives are even more fragmented.

This fragmentation of opposition, which increased further in 1987−8 when a faction within the SDP refused to join the new Social and Liberal Democrats, means that even though the Conservatives have only a minority share of the votes their position seems relatively secure. Curtice and Steed's analysis of the 1987 election results leads them to the conclusion that even tactical voting does not threaten the Conservatives. They argue that:

> Too few voters are readily prepared to switch their votes in the desired direction at a general election. The Conservatives will only lose their

majority in future if there is also an overall change in the distribution of party support (1988, p. 340).

Do developments of these kinds presage a long period of electoral hegemony for the Conservatives? That is certainly how some commentators and politicians interpret the current situation, but some caution needs to be exercised before reaching such a conclusion. In the first place, the extent of Conservative dominance in the last three elections should not be exaggerated. In each, their share of the vote was smaller than it was in 1970 and markedly lower than they achieved in the elections of the 1950s. The recent huge Conservative majorities in the House of Commons are products of a divided opposition and the operation of the electoral system rather than of great popularity among the voters. Secondly, there is no doubt that Mrs Thatcher has been, overall, an electoral asset for the Conservatives. But even she cannot go on for ever. At some point a new leader must take over, and it seems likely that there will be something of a succession problem since no one in the current Conservative leadership comes close to matching Mrs Thatcher in terms of flair, strength of personality and, one would guess, electoral appeal.

Thirdly, the effect of a strengthened centre party is double-edged. Although it divides opposition, it also makes defecting easier. Many Conservative voters would never dream of switching to Labour but could be tempted by the Democrats if they were unhappy with some aspect of government performance or policy.

Finally, the Conservatives, like the other parties, have suffered from the process of partisan dealignment. This is illustrated in Table 7.5. The

Table 7.5 Identification with Conservatives, 1964–87 (%)

	1964	1966	1970	Feb. 1974	Oct. 1974	1979	1983	1987
With Conservative identification	39	35	39	35	34	38	36	37
Proportion of Conservative identifiers who are 'very strong'	48	49	51	32	27	24	25	23

Sources: Sarlvik and Crewe (1983, pp. 334–7); 1983 BES data; 1987 BES data made available by Dr Heath.

percentage of the electorate identifying with the Conservatives has not varied a great deal since 1964. It is clear, however, that among these identifiers there has been a marked decline in the strength of their commitment to the party. By 1987 fewer than a quarter of Conservative identifiers were 'very strong' supporters of the party. The Conservatives have been successful in garnering votes at the last three elections but the electorate's commitment to the party is less than whole-hearted. If short-term factors such as the voters' preferences on issues or assessment of government performance begin to go against them, then votes could flow away from the Conservatives just as quickly as they flooded to them in 1979.

Early warning signs of this possibility were visible in the 1987 election. As noted in Chapter 4, Labour was the preferred party on three of the four most important issues in the election. In the event, the Conservatives' record in office saw them through, but governing a modern industrial society is complex and difficult, and all governments run into problems. It is possible that issues such as education, health and, in due course, the poll tax (which only Conservative MPs call the 'community charge'!) will begin to undermine the government's popularity. In addition, the Conservatives' trump card in terms of issues — defence policy — could be neutralised by developments between the superpowers in respect of arms reductions. Issue voting is volatile and unstable, and a run of bad luck at the wrong time might put the Conservatives in an awkward position electorally. It would be wrong to assume, then, that social change, a weak opposition and past success in government assure the Conservatives of continued electoral success in future.

Labour

It must be said, however, that the outlook for the Conservatives looks decidedly rosy when compared with the position in which the Labour party now finds itself. The 1983 election was a disaster for the party. There was some recovery in 1987 but in many ways that election served only to highlight Labour's electoral problems. In 1983 at least part of the blame could be put upon short-term difficulties such as an unpopular leader, a chaotic campaign organisation and an election manifesto which attracted much derision ('the longest suicide note in history', according to one senior Labour figure). In 1987, however, the party leader, Mr Kinnock, was much less unpopular and the campaign was highly professional. Yet Labour's recovery was modest, and was largely confined to Scotland, Wales and the North of England where an increase in votes could not bring large dividends in terms of seats, since they already held most of the constituencies they could realistically hope to win.

The causes of Labour's electoral problems are complex but three basic factors stand out. Firstly, in stark contrast to the Conservatives, social changes have worked against Labour. The social groups among whom Labour's appeal is strongest — manual workers, council tenants, workers in heavy industry, people who live in the North — are declining segments of the electorate. To have a chance of winning power Labour has to broaden its appeal and attract more support among the 'new' working class — homeowners, people living in the South and Midlands, and so on — as well as 'deepening' its support among traditional areas of strength. The importance of broadening the geographical base is emphasised by the fact that when constituency boundaries are next redrawn (as they must be at least every 15 years) there will inevitably be more constituencies in the South and fewer in the North (to take account of changes in population).

Secondly, class and partisan dealignment have had a particularly bad effect on Labour. Table 7.6 shows the trends in Labour party identification since 1964 and, in contrast to the Conservatives, the proportion of the electorate identifying with Labour has clearly declined. In the elections of 1983 and 1987 Labour fell behind the Conservatives for the first time in terms of this indicator of the level of basic support. In addition, even among the declining numbers of Labour identifiers, the proportion very strongly committed to the party has almost halved.

In the past, many people regularly voted Labour out of class and party loyalty even when they were lukewarm about, if not hostile to, Labour

Table 7.6 Identification with Labour, 1964−87 (%)

	1964	1966	1970	Feb. 1974	Oct. 1974	1979	1983	1987
With Labour identification	42	45	42	40	40	36	31	30
Proportion of Labour identifiers who are 'very strong'	51	50	47	41	36	29	28	26

Sources: As Table 7.5.

policies. As this kind of aligned voting has become less common, Labour's policies and performance have become more relevant to the voters' decisions and, on the whole, they do not appear to have been very impressed. Since it is unlikely that class and party loyalty will return to the levels of the 1950s and 1960s, it would appear the Labour's only option is to make its policies more attractive to the electorate.

The third problem is, however, that Labour's complicated party structure and decision-making processes — based on a commitment to a form of intra-party democracy which has to take account of affiliated trade unions as well as local constituency parties — make it difficult for the party leadership to respond quickly to problems. People who seek to modify policy are liable to be branded as 'careerists' or even 'traitors'. Labour leaders appear to spend a lot of their time coping with the internal politics of the party rather than working out what should be done about Labour's long-term electoral decline.

On the positive side, it is clear that the Labour party leadership does recognise these problems and realises that something has to be done about them. Policy reviews have been undertaken and even the commitment to unilateral nuclear disarmament — something of an albatross around the party's neck in recent elections — is being questioned. Important changes in the party's rules relating to such matters as the voting power of trade unions at the party conference and the direct participation of all members in internal party elections are being mooted. However, the extent to which the party as a whole can be persuaded to accept policy and institutional changes remains questionable.

Labour can also take some comfort from the fact that its support remains very solid in Scotland, Wales and the North of England. This geographical concentration means that even with a relatively small share of the vote nationally the party will still have a substantial number of seats in the House of Commons. In 1983 Labour was only narrowly ahead of the Alliance in terms of popular support, but won more than ten times as many seats. Labour consequently enjoyed the status of official Opposition and this brings many privileges in the conduct of business in the House, as well as extensive media coverage.

Labour's geographically concentrated support will enable it to remain a very substantial force in British politics for the foreseeable future. It is not even impossible that, given a favourable combination of short-term forces, Labour could win power or at least deny the Conservatives an overall majority. But the immediate outlook is bleak. In order to win an overall majority in the House of Commons at the next election, Labour requires an 8 per cent swing from the Conservatives (assuming other parties' votes are constant), and that is more than twice as great as they have achieved in any single election since 1945.

The Social and Liberal Democrats

Finally, what of the centre parties? In the two elections of 1983 and 1987, the SDP and the Liberals signally failed to 'break the mould' of British politics, although it might be said that they cracked it. The major hurdle which they faced, and failed to surmount, was the electoral system. The single-member, simple plurality system (or, more colloquially, 'first-past-the-post') rewards parties whose support is concentrated and penalises those whose support is evenly spread. A third party could get a respectable level of support in every constituency — say, 30 per cent of the vote — and yet fail to win a single seat. The Alliance vote, like that of the Liberals before 1983, was relatively similar among different social groups and, partly as a consequence of that, relatively even geographically. Across 22 geographical regions defined by Johnston et al. (1988, p. 35) the standard deviation of the Alliance share of the electorate was 3.8, compared with 8.9 and 10.0 for the Conservatives and Labour respectively. This made it difficult for the Alliance to convert voting support into seats and explains why more than 22 per cent of the vote won them only 3 per cent of seats.

Other features of Alliance voting made their position precarious. They lacked a substantial core support that could be relied upon and their voters were not strongly committed to the Alliance, viewing it, rather, as a vehicle for expressing disaffection from other parties. As Table 7.7 shows, basic identification with the Alliance parties increased somewhat in 1983 and 1987, but the percentage of the electorate identifying with the Alliance was still noticeably smaller than the shares of the votes they received in these elections. The level of 'very strong' commitment to the Alliance — always lower than in the cases of the other parties — indicates clearly that core support for the Alliance is rather small. In addition to these problems, Alliance voters in both 1983 and 1987 (like Liberal voters in previous elections) did not appear to share any distinctive set of policy positions or even a vague, general ideology.

There were signs in both 1983 and 1987, however, that the Alliance might have started to overcome some of these problems. Their 'retention rate' in both elections (the percentage of voters for a party at one election who also vote for it in a second election) was much greater than

Table 7.7 Identification with Liberals/Alliance, 1964−87

	1964	1966	1970	Feb. 1974	Oct. 1974	1979	1983	1987
With Liberal/Alliance identification	11	10	8	13	14	11	17	16
Proportion of Liberal/Alliance identifiers who are 'very strong'	32	35	26	12	14	14	21	10

Souces: As Table 7.5.
Note: For 1983 and 1987 the data refer to identification with the Liberals or the SDP or 'the Alliance'.

the Liberals used to achieve. And in 1983 Heath et al. (1985, Ch. 8) discerned a distinctive 'ideological space' which might in due course have formed a basis for regular Alliance voting.

Since the 1987 election, however, there have been major changes in the centre of British party politics. Immediately after the election, the question of a merger between the Liberals and the SDP was brought to the forefront of discussion. After much acrimonious debate, both parties voted to form a united Social and Liberal Democratic party. Opponents of merger in the SDP, led by David Owen, refused to join the new party, however, and kept a separate SDP in existence. Many Liberals were also hesitant about joining the Democrats (the shorthand name for the new party). The strains and divisions associated with the merger of the Alliance parties have not impressed the voters. Support for the third (and fourth) party in opinion polls fell to a level which is as low as it has been in the whole post-war period. The Democrats now appear to be back in the position that the Liberals were in before partisan and class dealignment opened up the opportunity for major electoral advances.

There is a glimmer of light for the Democrats, however. The continuing SDP is much weaker in terms of membership, councillors and party organisation at local level. SDP leaders give the impression of rather whistling in the dark, and it seems likely that the party will relatively quickly be consigned to the fringe of British politics while the Democrats become the recognised standard-bearers of the centre. Given that the electorate will remain dealigned, unstable and volatile, it is always possible that a combination of circumstances — the government becoming very unpopular, Labour continuing to be plagued by division and so on — and a measure of good luck might result in the Democrats finding themselves at the centre of another electoral revival for the political centre.

All of this is, of course, highly speculative. What is certain is that British electoral politics will continue to be more open and exciting than they were in the days of aligned voting. Dealignment and the rise of issue-related voting have created a situation in which the fortunes of the parties can alter very rapidly. Even the impression of stability given by three consecutive Conservative victories is misleading. The potential for rapid electoral change is greater than ever and that is why studying elections in the 1990s will continue to be interesting — as well as good fun.

Note

1. The BES figures reported in Table 3.3 suggest, however, that both groups swung from the Conservatives to Labour, −2 per cent in the case of non-manual workers and −1.5 per cent in the case of manual workers.

References

Anwar, M. (1986) *Race and Politics*, Tavistock Publications.

Beer, S. (1982) *Britain Against Itself*, Faber.

Benney, M., Gray, A.P. and Pear, R.H. (1956) *How People Vote*, Routledge & Kegan Paul.

Berelson, B., Lazarsfeld, P. and McPhee, W. (1954) *Voting*, University of Chicago Press.

Blumler, J.G. and McQuail, D. (1967) *Television in Politics*, Faber & Faber.

Bochel, J.M. and Denver, D. (1970) 'Religion and voting: a critical review and a new analysis', *Political Studies*, vol. 18, no. 2, pp. 205–19.

Bochel, J.M. and Denver, D. (1971) 'Canvassing, turnout and party support: an experiment', *British Journal of Political Science*, vol. 1, no. 3, pp. 257–69.

Butler, D.E. and Kavanagh, D. (1974) *The British General Election of February 1974*, Macmillan.

Butler, D.E. and Kavanagh, D. (1975) *The British General Election of October 1974*, Macmillan.

Butler, D.E. and Kavanagh, D. (1980) *The British General Election of 1979*, Macmillan.

Butler, D.E. and Kavanagh, D. (1984) *The British General Election of 1983*, Macmillan.

Butler, D.E. and Kavanagh, D. (1988) *The British General Election of 1987*, Macmillan.

Butler, D.E. and Pinto-Duschinsky, M. (1971) *The British General Election of 1970*, Macmillan.

Butler, D.E. and Stokes, D. (1969) *Political Change in Britain*, 1st edn, Macmillan.

Butler, D.E. and Stokes, D. (1974) *Political Change in Britain*, 2nd edn, Macmillan.

Campbell, A., Converse, P., Miller, W. and Stokes, D. (1960) *The American Voter*, John Wiley & Sons.

Central Statistical Office (1984) *Social Trends*, HMSO.

Crewe, I. (1981a) 'Why the Conservatives won; in H. Penniman (ed.) *Britain at the Polls 1979*, American Enterprise Institute, Washington.

Crewe, I. (1981b) 'Electoral participation', in D. Butler, H.R. Penniman and A. Ranney (eds) *Democracy at the Polls*, American Enterprise Institute, Washington.

Crewe, I. (1984) 'The electorate: partisan dealignment ten years on', in H. Berrington (ed.) *Change in British Politics*, Frank Cass & Co.

Crewe, I. (1985a) 'Great Britain', in I. Crewe and D. Denver (eds) *Electoral Change in Western Democracies*, Croom Helm.

Crewe, I. (1985b) 'How to win a landslide without really trying', in A. Ranney (ed.) *Britain at the Polls 1983*, American Enterprise Institute, Washington.

Crewe, I. (1986) 'On the death and resurrection of class voting: some comments on *How Britain Votes*', *Political Studies*, vol. 35, no. 4, pp. 620–38.

Crewe, I. (1987a) 'A new class of politics', *Guardian*, 15 June.

Crewe, I. (1987b) 'Tories prosper from a paradox', *Guardian*, 16 June.

Crewe, I., Fox, T. and Alt, J. (1977) 'Non-voting in British general elections 1966–October 1974', in C. Crouch (ed.) *British Political Sociology Yearbook*, vol. 3, Croom Helm.

Crewe, I. and Payne, C. (1971) 'Analysing the census data', in Butler and Pinto-Duschinsky (1971).

Crewe, I., Sarlvik, B. and Alt, J. (1977) 'Partisan dealignment in Britain 1964–1974', *British Journal of Political Science*, vol. 7, no. 2, pp. 129–90.

Curtice, J. and Steed, M. (1980) 'An analysis of the voting', in Butler and Kavanagh (1980).

Curtice, J. and Steed, M. (1982) 'Electoral choice and the production of governments: the changing operation of the electoral system in the UK since 1955', *British Journal of Political Science*, vol. 12, no. 3, pp. 249–98.

Curtice, J. and Steed, M. (1984) 'Analysis of the results', in Butler and Kavanagh (1984).

Curtice, J. and Steed, M. (1986) 'Proportionality and exaggeration in the British electoral system', *Electoral Studies*, vol. 5, no. 3, pp. 209–28.

Curtice, J. and Steed, M. (1988) 'Analysis', in Butler and Kavanagh (1988).

Denver, D. (1988) 'Predicting the next British election (or not, as the case may be)', *Parliamentary Affairs*, vol. 40, no. 2, pp. 238–49.

Denver, D. and Hands, G. (1974) 'Marginality and turnout in British general elections', *British Journal of Political Science*, vol. 4, no. 1, pp. 17–35.

Denver, D. and Hands, G. (1985) 'Marginality and turnout in British general elections in the 1970s', *British Journal of Political Science*, vol. 15, no. 4, pp. 381–8.

Downs, A. (1957) *An Economic Theory of Democracy*, Harper, New York.

Dunleavy, P. (1980) 'The political implications of sectoral cleavages and the growth of state employment', *Political Studies*, vol. 28, nos 3 and 4, pp. 364–83 and 527–49.

Dunleavy, P. (1987) 'Class dealignment in Britain revisited', *West European Politics*, vol. 10, no. 3, pp. 400–19.

Dunleavy, P. and Husbands, C.T. (1985) *British Democracy at the Crossroads*, George Allen & Unwin.

Eagles, M. and Erfle, S. (1989) 'Community cohesion and voter turnout', *British Journal of Political Science*, vol. 19, no. 1, pp. 115—25.

Franklin, M. (1985) *The Decline of Class Voting in Britain*, Oxford University Press.

Gallup (1987) *Gallup Political Index*, no. 323, July.

Glasgow University Media Group (1976) *Bad News*, Routledge & Kegan Paul.

Glasgow University Media Group (1980) *More Bad News*, Routledge & Kegan Paul.

Glasgow University Media Group (1982) *Really Bad News*, Writers and Authors Co-operative, London.

Goldthorpe, J.H., Lockwood, D., Bechhofer, F. and Platt, J. (1968) *The Affluent Worker*, 3 vols, Cambridge University Press.

Harrison, M. (1985) *TV News: Whose Bias?*, Policy Journals, Hermitage, Berks.

Harrop, M. (1982) 'Labour-voting conservatives: policy differences between the Labour party and Labour voters', in R. Worcester and M. Harrop (eds) *Political Communication: The General Election Campaign of 1979*, Allen & Unwin.

Harrop, M. (1986) 'Press coverage of post war British elections' in I. Crewe and M. Harrop (eds) *Political Communications: The General Election Campaign of 1983*, Cambridge University Press.

Heath, A., Jowell, R. and Curtice, J. (1985) *How Britain Votes*, Pergamon.

Heath, A., Jowell, R. and Curtice, J. (1987) 'Trendless fluctuation: a reply to Crewe', *Political Studies*, vol. 35, no. 2, pp. 256—77.

Heath, A., Jowell, R. and Curtice, J. (1988) 'Partisan dealignment revisited', paper presented at the Annual Conference of the Political Studies Association, Plymouth.

Heath, A. and McDonald, S. (1987) 'Social change and the future of the left', *Political Quarterly*, vol. 58, no. 4, pp. 364—77.

Johnston, R.J. and Pattie, C.J. (1988) 'Are we really all Alliance nowadays? Discriminating by discriminant analysis', *Electoral Studies*, vol. 7, no. 1, pp. 27—32.

Johnston, R.J., Pattie, C.J. and Allsop, J.G. (1988) *A Nation Dividing*, Longman.

Kavanagh, D. (1971) 'The deferential English: a comparative critique', *Government and Opposition*, vol. 6, no. 3, pp. 333—60.

King, A. (1975) 'Overload: problems of governing in the 1970s', *Political Studies*, vol. 23, nos. 2—3, pp. 284—96.

Lazarsfeld, P., Berelson, B. and Gaudet, H. (1968) *The People's Choice*, 3rd edn, first published 1944, Columbia University Press.

McAllister, I. and Rose, R. (1984) *The Nationwide Competition for Votes*, Frances Pinter.

McKenzie, R. and Silver, A. (1968) *Angels in Marble*, Heinemann.

McLean, I. (1973) 'The problem of proportionate swing', *Political Studies*, vol. 21, no. 1, pp. 57—63.

McLean, I. (1982) *Dealing in Votes*, Martin Robertson.

Mill, J.S. (1963) *Considerations on Representative Government*, World Classics edn, Oxford University Press.

Miller, W.L. (1977) *Electoral Dynamics*, Macmillan.

Miller, W.L. (1978) 'Social class and party choice in England: a new analysis', *British Journal of Political Science*, vol. 8, no. 3, pp. 257−84.

Miller, W.L. (1979) 'Class, region and strata at the British general election of 1979', *Parliamentary Affairs*, vol. 32, no. 4, pp. 376−82.

Miller, W., Broughton, D., Sonntag, N. and McLean, D. (1988) 'Political change in Britain during the 1987 campaign', paper presented at the Annual Conference of the Political Studies Association, Plymouth.

Milne, R.S. and MacKenzie, H.C. (1958) *Marginal Seat*, Hansard Society, London.

Mughan, A. (1986) *Party and Participation in British Elections*, Frances Pinter.

Nordlinger, E. (1967) *Working-Class Tories*, Macgibbon & Kee.

Norris, P. (1987) 'Four weeks of sound and fury . . . the 1987 British election campaign', *Parliamentary Affairs*, vol. 4, no. 4, pp. 458−67.

Parkin, F. (1967) 'Working-class Conservatives: a theory of political deviance', *British Journal of Sociology*, vol. 18, no. 3, pp. 278−90.

Pulzer, P.G. (1967) *Political Representation and Elections in Britain*, George Allen & Unwin.

Rose, R. (1974) 'Britain: simple abstractions and complex realities', in R. Rose (ed.) *Electoral Behaviour*, Free Press, New York.

Rose, R. (1980) 'Class does not equal party', Occasional Paper No. 74, Centre for the Study of Public Policy, University of Strathclyde.

Rose, R. (1985) 'Opinion polls as feedback mechanisms: from cavalry charge to electronic warfare', in A. Ranney (ed.) *Britain at the Polls 1983*, American Enterprise Institute, Washington.

Rose, R. and McAllister, I. (1986) *Voters Begin to Choose*, Sage, London.

Runciman, W.G. (1966) *Relative Deprivation and Social Justice*, Routledge & Kegan Paul.

Sarlvik, B. and Crewe, I. (1983) *Decade of Dealignment*, Cambridge University Press.

Startup, R. and Whittaker, E.T. (1982) *Introducing Social Statistics*, George Allen & Unwin.

Steed, M. (1966) 'An analysis of the results', in D. Butler and A. King, *The British General Election of 1966*, Macmillan.

Steed, M. (1986) 'The core−periphery dimension of British politics', *Political Geography Quarterly*, vol. 5, pp. 91−103.

Teer, F. and Spence, J.D. (1973) *Political Opinion Polls*, Hutchinson.

Trenaman, J. and McQuail, D. (1961) *Television and the Political Image*, Methuen.

Wallas, G. (1910) *Human Nature in Politics*, Constable & Co.

Whiteley, P. (1986) 'The accuracy and influence of the polls in the 1983 general election', in I. Crewe and M. Harrop (eds) *Political Communications: The 1983 Election Campaign*, Cambridge University Press.

Index